THE NEW YORK GIANTS
The Story of a Football Team

THE NEW YORK GIANTS

The Story of a Football Team

**Photographs by Dan Rubin,
official photographer, New York Giants**

Text by Al DeRogatis

DUELL, SLOAN AND PEARCE · NEW YORK

Affiliate of
MEREDITH PRESS
Des Moines & New York

Library of Congress Catalogue Card Number: 64-24481

MANUFACTURED IN THE UNITED STATES OF AMERICA FOR MEREDITH PRESS

To my wife Marilyn: Thanks for being so patient on those long Sunday afternoons.
DAN RUBIN

To my three girls—my wife, Louise, and my daughters Mary Ann and Diane.
I would also like to acknowledge the assistance of John Hess, executive editor of Meredith Press, an old football player himself, who helped in the preparation of this material.

AL DeROGATIS

CONTENTS

Dear Football Fans:

Anyone who has ever spent a Sunday afternoon at a professional football game will find hours of interesting and enjoyable reading in the pages that follow.

This is a book for the real pro football fan!

Dan Rubin, official photographer for the New York Giants, and Al DeRogatis, who was a great tackle with our club in the early 1950s, have teamed up to produce a fine study of the game.

Rubin's sideline photos bring all the action, all the drama, all the speed of football into focus right before your eyes. Dan is one of those photographers with a feel for the game, a fellow who knows where and when to aim his camera.

As a professional coach, I am always interested in Dan's pictures because they often show things that we can't see even on movie film. As an ordinary pro fan, I was delighted to peruse the collection of Rubin photos that appear on the following pages.

Al DeRogatis, who is still associated with the Giants, is a keen observer of our game. He has done a splendid job on the text that accompanies Rubin's art. I know I enjoyed reading his expert comments on the inside of pro football.

This is a first-class picture and word story of the National Football League and the Giants. I recommend it for everyone — coach, player and fan.

Sincerely,

Allie Sherman

Al Sherman
Head Coach
N.Y. FOOTBALL GIANTS

THE GIANTS

THIS BOOK is about an institution that is still very much alive — the New York Giants — so what I write now can be changed tomorrow — and probably will be. There have been histories of the Giants and countless record books compiled to tell every fan, until he has the blurs, what his favorites — Tittle, Gifford, Shofner, Chandler — have done since the beginning of time. Because these players are human, they are apt to improve or decline in ability. Football is too violent a sport to ever be static.

So this book is really a new kind of approach, and though it is about an institution, it is not intended to be a stodgy, official guide to football, containing objective facts that you can find in a number of places. It is an attempt to put into permanent form, for the moment, the action, the color, and the technical football information that I know many fans would like to have at their disposal. They have told me so.

I must confess that the book is biased,

for, as an alumnus of Mara Tech — as the Giants are sometimes called — I have certain loyalties, and they go pretty deep. So color your favorite pro eleven a deep shade of blue.

Over the last few years I have become increasingly intrigued with the growing knowledge that pro football fans — in and out of New York — have started to show. Because of my WNEW radio show here

in Manhattan, I have more than a passing opportunity to see and hear more people than I ever could as a player. These same fans are with it, in every respect, and I have to stay extremely awake to keep up with them. At banquets, coaches' clinics, communion breakfasts, and on countless other occasions I am constantly asked questions that show thought and previous experience with football. As our radio show continues to increase in popularity (we are now heard by approximately thirty million people on a game day) more and more questions come along that need careful thought and reasonably detailed answers.

Why not put these answers, or the best answers I can come up with, in some kind of usable shape, so that people can follow the game more closely than they

have before? But this information would have to be in a form that would be fun to read and general enough to apply to all phases of the professional game, with the Giants as prime examples, of course.

So here it is, far from a textbook, and personal as can be, from a former Giant who has acted as scout, spotter, and analyst for the last fifteen years. Ever since the days of the late Steve Owen and the umbrella defense, I have been watching those magic Sundays get better and better.

I think you will find that you can *use* this book, and you will be thrilled by the superlative photographs that Dan Rubin, the Giants' official photographer, has taken. We have even appended a special glossary to define those most-used technical terms that have added a whole new dimension to the English language. Knowing these special terms might even help your wife or girl-friend capture, for once, your complete attention on a Sunday afternoon. She might even learn something herself. However, you won't find any reports of secret conversations between one owner and another back in

1927, no locker-room exposés that will revolutionize tomorrow's sports page; but you might see what makes the Giants go.

The Giants, in the last eight years, have been enjoying a run of success that many wonder about. Will it last? Who knows, but in sports the past is definitely prologue. The whole story has not always been that pleasant. There has been some definite black mixed with that special shade of blue.

Back in 1925, when the late T. J. Mara bought the Giants' franchise for five hundred dollars, rumor has it that he would have much more quickly bought Gene Tunney — if he had had the chance. From this modest and less than flattering beginning, the Giants have prospered to an extent that even astounds T. J.'s two sons, Jack and Wellington. In other words, it has been a human, growing thing. That the Giants have had only three coaches since 1930 might account for an important part of this. When Steve Owen died just last spring, he was still watching for new talent, trying to help Allie Sherman and the rest of the squad in the hard-won but essentially matchless success they have enjoyed in the National Football League. Since 1956, when they beat the Bears for the league title, the Giants have won Eastern Championships in 1958, 1959, 1961, 1962, and 1963. And this good fortune has not spoiled their hopes for more. As all heads turn to New York in so many other areas of national interest, so do NFL football fans follow every move the New York Giants make — some with slight malice, others with glee.

4

The team has survived the onslaught of the war, the competition of the All-America Conference in the late 1940's, and the recently assertive and steadily growing neighbor of the 1960's: the American Football League. Oddly enough, New Yorkers are very frank about many aspects of the special world they are sure they inhabit, and they are simply snobs about the Giants. Their boys have class and color, and they are fun to watch. If it is gauche to whistle and stamp and holler for their favorites, New Yorkers are going to let the chips fall, at least this one time: they are going to *show* their affection and loyalty for a change.

And they have been showing it. The motel reservations in Bridgeport, Connecticut, for a home game (when the local New York area is blacked out) resemble the Iowa City, Iowa, countryside before the big game with Minnesota. And Red Bank, New Jersey, has more stadium parties — that never get away from the living room — than Ann Arbor, Michigan, before the traditional battle with Ohio State.

There is a reason behind most of it. The Giants have been consistently winning, and, interestingly enough, winning with style. Their offense has been filled with the thrilling runs and passes that make the game a bona fide gas most of the time. No more slow-moving formality for today's fans; give them action and technical proficiency. And the Giants have been obliging, we must admit that.

One reason that the Giants have been doing so well, in my opinion, is that their management is as professional as it ex-

pects its players to be. Smart trades have been made; sometimes favorite players have been moved around, but even the favorite player will often admit that the trade, the very one that involved him, made sense. And no one in the Giants' organization gets down on a player very easily, either. This is something that all pros — old and young — come to know eventually. You can have a great season, then fall on your ear, and it's good-by — with a lot of clubs. There is a definite heritage in the Giants' organization, specifically, *to win,* but to protect your own in doing so. As Joe Walton said a few seasons ago during a hot training-camp session in Fairfield, Connecticut, "Hell, playing for the Giants, even in this damned sun, is fun!" And he meant it.

It has been fun — for Joe, and for the people who pay to watch him. Never has it been harder to get tickets, and never has the radio-TV income been greater. But I agree with the NFL management that unrestricted TV would easily put professional football in the same spot that baseball got into due to unrestricted

5

coverage of the game. If season tickets are hard to come by, the product is obviously a good one. And here is consolation: all the road games are available to New York fans. The spectre of falling attendance in the face of unrestricted TV exposure could become a real problem. Then, with coverage always available and gate receipts declining, it would be nearly impossible for the Giants and other NFL clubs to reinstate previously existing restrictions.

I do think the championship game, now often played in weather fit for Kodiak bears (not even Chicago ones), should be shifted to a warmer site. The fans should be polled, of course, but I think they would agree — and that they would see better football.

The problems are many, but I think the Giants' management has handled them well. It has created a place that is thrilling to visit and one that puts on the best show in town — on any given autumn Sunday at 2:05 P.M.

This sweet smell of success has come back to haunt the Giants in an ironic and very real way. No other team has been associated with quite as many leaders as have the Giants. For example: Steve Owen, Jim Lee Howell, Allie Sherman, Andy Robustelli, Ed Kolman in New York and Vince Lombardi at Green Bay, Harland Svare for the Los Angeles Rams, Tom Landry at Dallas, and so on. The list will undoubtedly get bigger.

I think some of the examples of the frenzy that has gripped the modern pro fan are worth noting here. They are constantly being called to my attention. Not unsurprisingly, I hope it all grows immeasurably.

Here are some specifics: On any Sunday of a Giants' home game during the season, Frank O'Keefe of White Plains, New York, a calm, level-headed businessman who works hard, loves his family, goes to PTA meetings, and is faithful to his wife, becomes a man on fire, a fiend driven by a compulsive madness that has now affected millions of people up and down the eastern seaboard.

On Sundays, Frank schedules his whole life around the football games of the New York Giants. He eats, sleeps, breathes Giants, addresses his family in a slight daze, hurries to a predestined meeting place with several of his friends and neighbors before going to his regular box seat in Yankee Stadium. His wife, and the other wives of his group, grab their husbands after the game, whenever and wherever they can. It is their only hope for a Sunday meeting.

Before the Giants-Chicago Bears championship game last winter, two seventy-five-year-old ladies from Red Bank, New Jersey, chartered a small airplane and flew to Kennedy Airport and from there, in the foulest of weather, to Chicago, where, after a sleepless night, they checked into a hotel close to the Giant camp, then accompanied those Giants who happened to be Roman Catholics to Mass that Sunday morning — all this in order to see that their boys did the right thing: beat those blasted Bears. The husbands of these determined women did not go into the air for this one. They might have been killed.

A recent will filed for probate by an attorney in Connecticut listed, among other assets, a season-ticket subscription to the Giants' games. The American Way of Death, and I mean this seriously, is not going to cheat one's friends and relatives out of enjoying a good Sunday's fun in the name of the deceased.

There is a madness in the land, a compulsion that has become all-consuming for millions of otherwise law-abiding people. They have become hooked on the game of professional football — a game that combines the raw power of the Roman Colosseum with the traditional finesse of the ballet.

Never before have so many people known so surely one thing about a sport: they never will have to stand still for a dull moment. In case the game is slow — wait, it will change, just like the weather. The action is fast, the socking is good, and the technical proficiency unparalleled in the history of sports.

The New York Giants have dominated their environment, and they have made countless people aware that the blitz might not have been invented in World War II. In short, they have established a regime that is hard to duplicate and define, but impossible to overlook.

There is something about watching the Giants take the field these days that spells authority — the knowledge that you be-long on that green turf of the stadium, that you know what you're doing. In short, a professional *élan*.

What sort of fellow is he, this strange mixture of brawn and skill, this muscled giant who moves as if he'd studied with Balanchine? Well, he's not stupid. No matter where he went to school (and almost all of the players I've known since my years at Duke did go to college), he can't be lazy or careless or not do his homework. The competition is too tough; he would not last in this business if he didn't work at it — mentally and physically. The plays themselves, with their many variations, are too complex, the pressure of others coming along too intense to allow for idle, shiftless behavior. The higher brain centers are involved, a psychologist might say, and he'd be right. But the lower centers are involved too — good arms and legs.

But above all — and I repeat this whenever anyone puts the question — the professional football player has great *pride* in his work, in his profession. He has worked too long and too hard to put it all down lightly. Millions of people, through what many have referred to as "the magic of radio and television," have also got their eyes glued firmly on what the professional football player does. Also, to his great sorrow — and sometimes his joy — the game movies are played and played and replayed by a vigilant coaching staff.

Still, the pressures and the satisfactions are mostly internal. For example, Frank

Gifford was badly hurt by that crushing tackle that Chuck Bednarik put on him toward the end of the 1960 season. Frank had been a star for years. He could have quit, knowing that he had put real accomplishments beside his name. He had to apologize to no one. As all the sporting world knows, he sat out the 1961 season. He was hooked, too, just as his admirers were. He was determined to close his career with a triumph — and not by being carried unconscious from the field. He took a big chance, and he won. But I don't think Frank really had a choice. He *had* to come back.

I can think of many other examples from my playing days. Em Tunnell's cool reception in the office of the Giants was not a reflection on Mr. Mara. Nobody knew who he was. He had been a steady performer at Iowa under Eddie Anderson, but an unscouted one. As reported often before, Em told the Giants management that he could help, he could make the grade — which he did. For more than ten years after that he roamed the defensive backfield of the Giants, setting records and defying the odds. He was too old, they said, and he knew it sometimes when Monday morning rolled around. But he didn't quit, either. Now he's the Giants game scout, one of the best in the NFL.

The sum of it all is that a professional — a Giant — gives his best when the worst is expected. The oldest saw in sports is the phrase, "When the going gets tough, the tough get going." I don't know how to put it better, and I won't try. Above all, the pro knows he has a lot to lose and a lot to gain. But that's only secondary. He's got himself to face that next day, and for the best kind of player, that's the hardest puss in the world to stare down.

Above all, the pro knows he can make a good living for himself, make a fine reputation, and, if he's good at his job, he'll be remembered. Selling insurance (as I do), or modeling sports shirts — all can come out of it. But nothing really comes out if there isn't a great desire to be first right from the start. Many people ask me if it's not hard to sustain the intangible quality of spirit and fight after college. Of course it is, but I've never seen a man stick yet who just played for the pay check. He has something else going for him every time. He's got great physical ability, surely, but he's also got a big something that isometrics or any other exercise never added to the equipment of a player — it's called heart by many and guts by some and fight by others. I like to call it style. Someone else called it grace under pressure. One sure thing is that there are a lot of words to describe it, and only one way to show it — in action.

As Louis Armstrong (an old pro himself) once said to a breathless admirer who had been asking him what jazz really meant, what it was all about: "Daddy, you been standin' there lissenin' to me play. If you don't know now, I can't tell you." Well, I can, and I'd love to. That's what this book is all about.

TALENT SCOUTING

As someone who has been close to the Giants for many years, I'm often asked how they get their players. What is the secret system that permits them to go on filling that vacant spot often with just the right kind of player?

There is no secret society, no esoteric rite that all of us engage in to pick just that right man. Every club in the National Football League has a system, and most of them are very similar to the Giants'.

I'd be the first to admit, though, that the system, though not secret and sinister, is highly detailed and exceptionally thorough. Here's how it is set up:

The Giants' coaches are, of course, the key members of the scouting organization, organized with territory and individual specialty in mind. For instance, Personnel Director Jim Lee Howell, former Giants' coach, works colleges from the Mississippi River east, covering many small schools that not many fans have heard of but which produce many fine,

even exceptional, football players. Why this is such a common occurrence nowadays will be described later. Peahead Walker, another Giant, covers the schools in the South. He works closely with Em Tunnell, who is, of course, the Giants' game scout during the season. Tunnell works most closely with Negro colleges throughout the country. I handle those schools which are located in the East and those around the game sites of the Giants.

This geographical distribution of experienced scouts looking for promising talent is just a start. There are many other details that, for obvious reasons, we won't go into here. There is a plan, however, and the plan is carried out throughout the year. Reports are filed (and they are extensive), so that the wisest choices can be made when draft time rolls around.

Lately, the Giants have been winning championships pretty consistently, so their first choices have been long gone before their turn rolls around. (Unfortunately, other teams have good scouts, too, and they always seem to be trying to get the best men away from us. We are frankly prejudiced and have told our competitors so. This has not stopped their campaign.)

The winning club, of course, picks last in the college draft. The last place club, as things are set up now, gets first choice. This system has been devised in order to provide for an orderly redistribution of talent and proficiency around the league. And I think that the plan is fair and basically good for the league and the players involved.

I should say that one rule has always existed in my handling of the recruiting responsibility: I will not contact a boy until he becomes eligible for the professional draft. I never approach an athlete before he graduates — or before his college class has moved forward to a point where the individual player is eligible to become a professional, even though he himself has not graduated.

The most frequent questions I've had to answer for some time, at banquets and coaching clinics, have been about small schools and the unusual amount of really talented players that they produce. All I can say is that it seems to be a question decided largely four years before the player becomes a pro. Because of the stiff educational standards of many of the well-known schools around the country, the physically gifted, but perhaps scholastically less advanced, athlete at-

tends a school that has a slightly lower academic requirement for entrance. He then goes on to star in a conference that does not fully test his tremendous natural skills.

This kind of player does present a rather unique problem to his pro coaches when he goes to his first summer camp. He may be physically a giant and have great natural equipment, but his previous coaching level might have been slightly unsophisticated. He played on his instinct, and he must therefore react and adjust to a great range of detailed coaching. Often simple terms for certain blocking maneuvers may be entirely unknown to a player of this type. Usually, his above-average gifts will pull him through, but he has a big intellectual adjustment to make, a much more complicated discipline to learn before starting off in the NFL.

Something should also be said for the importance of individual skills in our brand of football, as compared with that of today's colleges. The individual specialist — the kicker, passer, or pass catcher — can be most outstanding in his own way in college, yet play on a consistently losing team. He simply did not have the equivalent backing-up that he is bound to get on a team like the Giants.

I'm often put under mild pressure to tell the funniest scouting story I know. The one that keeps coming back concerns a day at the University of Notre

Dame, in South Bend, Indiana. I was there to cover a certain well-known backfield star, and I found myself sitting next to an amiable Irishman who kept singing the praises of a substitute Notre Dame back. The man explained vigorously to me, after I had asked him why his favorite was not starting, that the kid *had* it — and that everybody would see when he got in there and mixed it up. The game began, and soon our friend pointed excitedly to a Notre Dame substitution. His favorite was going into the Notre Dame defensive backfield. I looked up from my scouting chart to see the boy intercept a pass on the first play he was in the game. The man next to me jumped up and down and screamed, "That's my son! I knew he could do it."

On the next series of downs, this particular young man let a punt get behind him, and he never returned to the Irish line-up. It was a very quiet bench next to me for the rest of the afternoon. The moral in this little story is that I naturally get a lot of tips each year, as do all the Giants scouts, about good and semigood boys — in every part of the country. And each one of these leads is checked out. Often professional teams can gain much information by using the routine mail questionnaire that is sent to the larger schools. Many times a former coach or associate of the Giants will call the front office directly about a prospect that shows special promise. Of course, this kind of

personal, dependable network of intelligence must be well-organized and reliable. But nothing can be overlooked — not even our rather emotional father who merely wanted his son to get the attention that he deserved.

No matter how a boy is found, he must prove his ability to the scout who does finally see him. What we look for can be fairly easily described. First of all, the player must be *dominant,* a champion in attitude as well as execution. I suppose the easiest way to put it is that he is in charge — of himself and the situation, at all times. This kind of player usually has a good mind, makes very few mental errors, and is in strong physical condition. The days of the college star who can drink a case of beer, stay out until 5 A.M., then come through with the big play against State are generally over.

Above all, the kind of man we look for is stable and has good instinct. He just naturally does the right thing. And this doesn't mean that all good pro players are just superior specimens. Many didn't have that great natural ability to do the right thing. But they developed the right habits — as Allie Sherman would say, to sustain themselves.

For example, I was sent to cover a game that West Virginia was playing some years ago, to watch a man who now would not mean a great deal to many fans. Instead of signing that man, I came up with a fellow named Sam Huff. Sam

11

was persistent, he had the courage to *lose* as well as win. He had, for want of a better word, purpose. The good winner, as we like to call him, takes a *loss* the hardest of anyone. He's playing for keeps, and he expects the same from his follows — professional or college. And this kind of expression can be quickly communicated to an experienced scout who may not be looking for that particular player at all at the start of the game. But you can bet the scout has filled his book with notes by the end. That's what I did with Sam.

There is a constant battle raging among many fans concerning the "best" area of the country for pro talent. I don't happen to believe in sticking my entire neck out like this, but I will hazard a few guesses, based on my experience with Giants' teams going back to the early 1950's.

I think the Big Ten is still in first place as far as numbers are concerned. But the Conference is being hard pressed to maintain this position. Recruiting competition, higher academic standards — many factors are responsible for this condition. In the general geographic area represented by the Big Ten, there are several "favorite" schools which most scouts look at rather closely. Although it is not in the Big Ten, I'd have to place Notre Dame in a very key spot in this kind of analysis, even though its record lately has not been equal to the great postwar teams that pro-

duced Lujack, Sitko, Hart, and many others. Next, Michigan State has been closely watched in the last several years — and rightly so. It has turned out some fine competitors. Ohio State, where the familiar question, "What players shall we play this year?" is still asked, has been most productive. Jim Parker of the Baltimore Colts has been giving fits to the defensive platoons around our league since he left Columbus in the mid-fifties. And then there was a bothersome little guy named Hopalong Cassidy.

The Southwest, with its fine tradition of wide-open passing, has to be carefully watched, for some of the finest throwing arms in the NFL have come from this region. Sammy Baugh perhaps started it all, and some slightly unreasonable Giant fans might feel that a guy named Y. A. Tittle ends it all, too.

In the South, you must pay close attention and tribute to the fine interior linemen and pass-catching ends. The style of football in this area has something to do with it, of course. The tradition of Tennessee, for instance, and its powerful lines cannot be overlooked by a scout. There have been many good linemen from Tennessee, because there was a predictable, regular fund of talent here.

Much of our scouting activity is based on this tricky, but nevertheless real belief in tradition, the ability of one coach or one kind of offensive formation to produce many of the players we must have.

12

The reputation of a particular coach or a particular school cannot be disregarded.

I've already noted the apparent ironic abundance of talent turned out by small, obscure schools, often in remote sections of the United States, sometimes greatly in need of even the most basic coaching techniques. Roosevelt Brown is just such an example. The simplest blocking positions and moves had to be learned in Rosey's first summer training camp. But he had such physical endowment, and such pride in making the team, that he overcame his handicap. Many others do the same thing.

Aside from these important questions of area and reputation, the most critical factor influencing our scouting decisions is need — what the Giants are currently searching for in a special type of player for a specific position. An additional runner has been necessary for some time in the Giants' backfield, as well as replacements for soon-departing veterans — both needs are always going to influence where we go to watch, whom we look for — and whom we bring back.

If I can prescribe, for a moment, the major needs that face the Giants, as this is being written, they are: a top runner, a clarification of Glynn Griffing's position as Tittle's successor, a good blocking tackle, an interior defensive man, a corner linebacker, and one more deep defensive man. These needs are constantly changing (and some of them might have been solved before you read this). No team is going to call its house perfectly in order. The game is too tough, the competition too ruthless for that.

The men who are signed and brought to camp as a result of our scouting work must prove their right to be Giants. Those who do not present, perhaps, one of the most delicate decisions the coaches and eventually Sherman must make all season.

The Giants summer training camp will see some who will make the team and play a great deal during their first season. Others will show real promise but will not be regarded as ready for the team to take them on formally. They may well become part of the taxi squad, a group of young players who stay with the Giants through the season, but who do not dress for the games. Their weeks during the regular season are spent in running opposition plays, getting the feel of the Giants organization, its way of doing business. One outstanding product of this system, one who might otherwise have been absent when his big opportunity came along, is Jerry Hillebrand, who this year is expected to fill the rather large vacancy of Sam Huff.

After scouting is completed, for the moment, the rookie begins to show whether he makes the first squad, stays with the taxi contingent, or is released before the season starts. In any event, he will know he's been through a long, hot summer.

TRAINING CAMP

As MILLIONS of Americans prepare for deserved vacations, as others curse the heat of their deprived urban existence, professional football players begin gathering for that ordeal in the sun, the summer training camp. From about the middle of July to the latter part of

August, a great deal of the planning and careful thought of the entire coaching staff is put into action — and more intramural body contact can be seen then than during the entire balance of the season.

The double practice sessions, the sometimes unbearable heat — all can be punishing for anyone, including pro football players. But the exercises and the constant repetition of offensive and defensive maneuvers can be the real key to success in the regular season. No football player in his right mind ever liked *all* of it, but he does realize that it is crucial to his and the team's eventual success or failure.

The rookies, receivers, passers, and position "switchers" usually report about a week early under the Giants system, in order to work on their assignments under very close personal supervision of the coaching staff. The Giants actually divide personnel into two levels of competence: rookies and other new men, and the veterans from last year's club. Heavy emphasis is placed on conditioning during these days. For example, the use of isometrics has been increasing lately, and there are the expected drills on running. Timing, which is so important in the regular season, gets more work than almost anything else. Plays are run so many times that the offense, sore as it is in muscles that might be far from perfect yet, comes close to quiet rebellion from time to time. But, as Allie Sherman says, "We must *establish* during this time. Basic language and technique must be repeated so often that they will become second nature."

Some drills and exercises that were once thought to be so important have gone completely from the professional's repertoire. Duck walking, that awkward and often painful squatting movement that hopefully strengthens muscles, is now gone. (I just came along a little too early.)

But the pros do not pass the fundamentals by. Football, as someone once pointed out, is still a game of hitting the other fellow harder than he hits you.

As a result, Allie spends a lot of time on basic blocking and tackling drills during those opening days. After conditioning is as close to perfection and as certain as it can reasonably be, contact begins — usually about a week after the full squad is assembled. This contact and the injuries that might result are taken quite seriously. As a matter of fact, every man has his ankles taped. He also tends to any injury he may have. Failure to do this results in an automatic twenty-five-to-fifty-dollar fine.

The men all live together in dormitories at training camp, though some of them who live close enough can go home. Joe Walton is one example, since

Stamford, Connecticut, is so very close. But most of the players, after a morning workout, for instance, glide quietly to their rooms and move softly between the bedsheets. They are not hiding, just trying to summon enough energy to face the afternoon.

But it is not all complete drudgery. If there weren't some joy in hitting an opponent, the game wouldn't be any fun at all, but the joy usually increases in direct proportion to the ability of the body to get in shape. Allie has one important motto for this time: "Work hard, but leave them laughing," meaning never practice so long that the session becomes a dreaded torture to the players. Some coaches have prided themselves on three- and four-hour sessions — to toughen the boys — but Allie never works the Giants more than one hour and twenty minutes at a time.

Over-all, during this time Sherman is trying to build his basic offense. During the off-season, he has experimented, at least in the abstract, with his next season's material, his strengths and weaknesses — so often that he knows exactly what he has to do now that the living material is before him. Allie, like all NFL coaches, could put Darryl Zanuck in the shade as far as watching that moving-picture machine. Sherman and his staff have studied each game of the previous season hundreds of times in order to gauge their next season's attack and to plan their basic defenses.

Also, the defensive holes must be plugged during training camp. There just isn't time to try this during the regular season. Of course, the rookies and last year's taxi-squad members have been closely evaluated with these weaknesses in mind. Now is their chance to prove themselves — to see if they can live up to the plans that the coaching staff has made for them. Old wounds must be examined with the coolest of minds. Players with serious physical injuries from previous seasons still have to be tested, under complete game conditions, to see if they can go the route this year. This test is often a cruel and exacting one.

Above all, these days are a time for working on perfection — on the timing and patterns that a good offense and defense must turn to automatically in the heat of the season. Defensive backs will find themselves walking backwards in their sleep because they've been doing nothing else during their waking hours. Offensive men will come out of the shower every morning in a crouch, because they've charged so often during the previous day that they now do it instinctively. It is a tough time, in many ways, but a satisfying one. If one makes the team or keeps his old job under the heaviest threat of a newcomer, he can

16

legitimately wallow in his triumph. It can be a lonely time, too, especially for the rookie, for no one is going to give up an established position easily. Most veterans do not look forward to seeing their old friends (and their friends' families) looking for work elsewhere. The Giants have their Establishment, just as there is one in almost every organization, and a man earns his way into it.

In order to build the offense around his basic strength, Sherman must test it in these early days as soon as possible. After about a week and a half of twice-a-day drills, the first scrimmage is held. Complete game conditions will prevail after the third week, except for the absence of kickoffs and punt returns, the most dangerous plays in the game as far as injuries are concerned.

Twice-a-day drills are usually stopped at the end of the third week, and one-a-day sessions will be the rule until the first exhibition game, which usually takes place about August 15. Don't think that the Giants take these exhibitions lightly. "This is a game of habit," says Sherman, "and preseason form will show our season

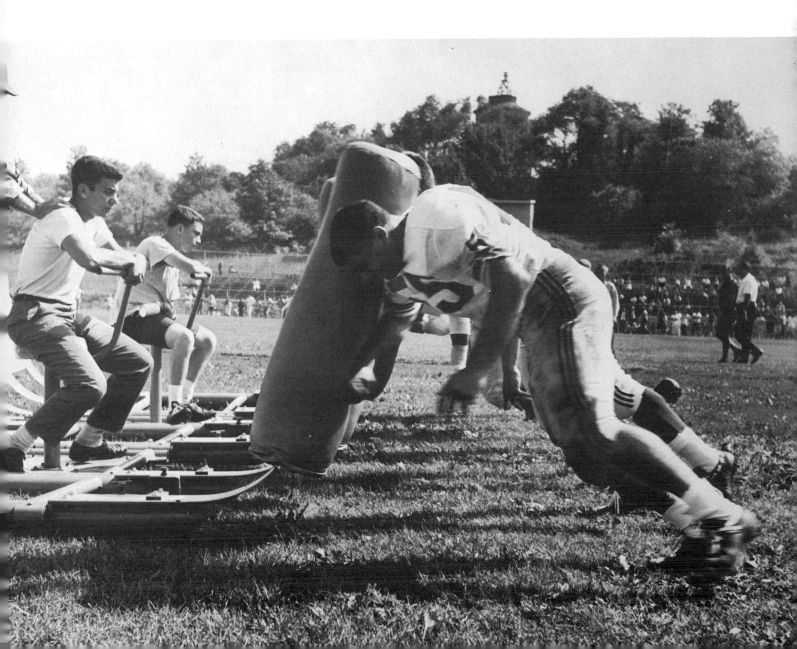

quality — or lack of it. Winning those games also builds confidence and that important momentum that thrusts you into a winning season."

Each player is given what we call a Play Book. He is expected to fill it with the basic information that he needs to play his particular position. As the sessions continue, he is expected to add all the details that give him a sophisticated knowledge of everything he will need to know. The individual play is specifically outlined, but in addition he will have to assimilate as soon as possible the complexities of the automatic call as it affects his job and the entire basic philosophy behind the Giants offensive thinking. The Play Book is the Bible of training camp, but it is far from an unalterable text; the book is constantly changing and being expanded. There might be one hundred variations on, let's say, twenty-five basic

plays to be used throughout the season, and each one must be committed to memory.

But as so many players have pointed out to me over the years, especially those traded from other teams, the Giants summer practice can be fun. Specialties are sharpened, skills are exercised constantly. And if a man is really good at what he's doing (passing, punting, knocking down passes), he's going to enjoy doing it. As we've said, Allie believes strongly in a short, well-defined session in which the work is crisp and exciting and never dull. The energies that are put out needlessly in practice never get exercised in the game.

You might get a little tired of hearing Greg Larson's muscle-building apparatus being dragged over the floor above you (one wag called it "Life in the Inner Sanctum"), or you might have sore legs and a sore stomach for a while, but eventually you get to like it. You're doing what you do for a living in this world, your profession, and you're going to do it as best you can. There is an 11 P.M. curfew, and you can't drink anything stronger than beer, but this kind of discipline has never really killed anyone. The training-table food is good, if simple, and the life may be a little monastic for those who can't get home. But the time does pass swiftly, and the excitement of the approaching season soon grabs everyone.

As many as ten thousand fans are apt to show up at the Fairfield training quarters for some scrimmages, so game conditions are with you almost right from

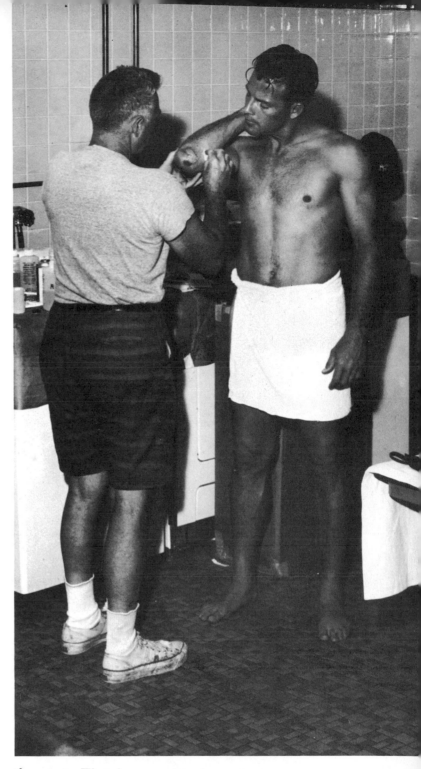

the start. There's a saying in summer camp that a veteran can be awfully tough in August, and it's very true. But then a rookie, especially a hungry one, can be, too. This makes for the best Pier Six brawls in August that you could possibly see. And it's only the beginning of the

19

20

long race for the big marbles. What's done here, in semisecluded heat, can produce very real results before millions of fans, those actually physically present and those ardent TV customers, in the bitter cold of December.

Each day a schedule of all activities is issued. Each minute is accounted for. On the field a horn blows at a scheduled time, calling different groups together, sending others to far corners of the field. There is a pervasive atmosphere of serious business, but there's room for some fun, too, as we said. Y. A. Tittle is famous for his early-morning calls to breakfast, which pester the rest of the team. He has been coming to training camp for a long time, but he rarely tires of it. These little gestures from the veterans usually break up the routine and the tension, and they are especially good for everyone's morale. Fellows like Gifford and Tittle are so friendly to the rookies that they will even play a little poker with them, pausing to take a young man's money if he cares to part with it.

In between the ubiquitous horn blowing and the off-field relaxation, such drills as working on the two-man blocking sled are put into effect. The forearm shiver is a regular drill, as is the endless running, at this time especially, to bring back that perhaps slightly deserted wind.

Above all, the Giants' summer practice is well-planned and well-defined. Allie has a favorite word: execution. And he works like hell to make sure that the word is transformed into action. That first week may see a lot of stiffness and pain, but by the third week men are really moving out and enjoying it.

There are the usual anxieties. One year it might be Tom Scott's concern for his old arm injury. Will it stand up this time? Will it be too serious for him to continue? Frank Gifford, when he came back to camp in 1962, had the biggest of questions facing him. What happens if he gets hit and the head injury means a complete blackout? But these real and dangerous possibilities must be forgotten. The careful man is often the injured man. A commitment

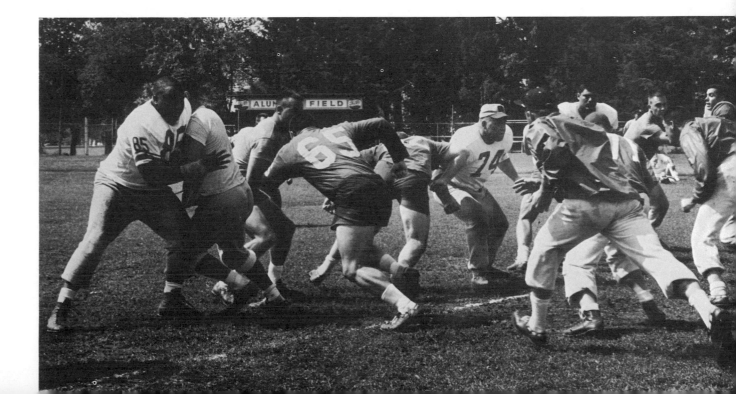

must be made, and then the action must follow. Not many flinching linemen or cake-walking halfbacks have made it in the NFL.

Unfortunately, the time must come to cut the squad. Rookies, sometimes well-known and well-publicized ones, are often casualties. Because of the intense effort that these men have made, the coaching staff's decisions are particularly hard. But in reality, and this isn't rationalizing, it's better to tell a man right away rather than have him spend one unproductive year with the Giants — one not leading anywhere — that will delay his beginning whatever *right* business career he may choose.

And let's face it: many are called but few are chosen. The key seems to be that the major athlete, the real pro, will always have enough concentration to keep himself in top physical and mental condition at all times. He has a sufficient mentality and presence to keep himself fit in the off-season, too, so that he comes to camp in complete control of himself and the situation. He's aware of what he must do to meet the competition each year, and he has enough pride and inner drive to make himself meet this challenge.

Pruning the squad is delicate work, and the entire coaching staff has contributed to the final decisions about everyone, All-Americans or relatively unknown players.

22

HOW THE WEEK GOES

THE QUESTION often comes up about a typical Giants week during the season. How does the team get ready for the next opponent? How does it profit from the game played the previous Sunday? How does it feel to look at movies that might not be flattering to a player's ego?

Order and regularity are the marks of any professional's craft. And it's the same with the Giants — only more so. On Monday, for example, the players' day off, the coaches probably have their toughest work day. The game films are studied religiously, to spot flaws in the offense, to tighten defensive weaknesses that might be particularly vulnerable to the following Sunday's opponent. Unfortunately, the films are not always as pleasant as watching Elizabeth Taylor in her latest effort. The same play, if it's particularly important or revealing, will be shown hundreds of times — backward and forward — to get the slightest insight into a new idea, a new adjustment that could mean touchdowns in the games to come. It is a tired staff that returns home in the small hours of Tuesday morning, but it is one that is ready — fully prepared to start the next day activating the game plan which Allie has devised.

Tuesday sees the bruised and still-tired team assembling for a loosening-up session, with emphasis on watching the game films in segments — offense watching its specialty and the defense doing likewise. There is nothing as satisfying as seeing your epic block immortalized for all the world to see, and nothing quite as agonizing as perhaps having a missed block, one that caused real damage, being pointed out for your benefit — over and over — for all your good buddies to howl over and endure with you. Slowly, however, plans are shaping for the next Sunday. The tension begins to mount as the triumphs or the reversals of the past get lost in the always hopeful tomorrow that means next Sunday.

By Wednesday, the game plan is clearly in mind. Now the job is to put it into action, into *execution,* to return to that favorite Sherman term. In addition to the drill on the field (the familiar one hour and twenty minutes), the team watches the movie of the next opponent's last game. The NFL rule currently states that films of the last two games of the next opponent can be exchanged. This regulation makes for an organized and extremely detailed way of preparation. Gone are the days when a revolutionary, last-minute change meant complete confusion for old Siwash as State revised its entire attack, using that secret weapon that fools everyone at Homecoming. Still, there are ways to change and to adapt in a week's time. However, no group of men, to my knowledge, is as fully prepared for the job to be done as the NFL teams are. Their records would bear me out.

On Thursdays there is a heavy drill, too. There is no contact during a typical week of the season, at least contact that could count under regular game conditions. Running is emphasized, and there is a minute breakdown as far as position-by-position analysis is concerned. Defense works on the particular running and passing threats posed by the next opponent, and the offense works against the opponent's defensive patterns. The taxi squad becomes adept, week by week, at imitating everyone else's plays, and they repeat and repeat, so that no surprise is possible.

During the week, the Giants work as two entirely separate teams — offense and defense — concentrating on things done badly the week before. There are no full uniforms in view, of course, but some players may wear shoulder pads and a helmet to get accustomed to game conditions as much as possible. The basic game plan is also polished — the basic plays with all their variations, which hopefully will be used to perfection the following week. I say "perfection" because they are practiced so much that the players react to them by pure instinct. There can't be any doubts or hesitations — the battle simply cannot be won if there are.

By Friday the Giants are just about through polishing the game plan. They constantly work for this perfect "execution," which Allie expects at all times. By this day there should be very few

mental errors. If there are many errors, something is drastically wrong, and immediate adjustment is made. There are still ways to improve blocking positions, for example, or offensive maneuvers.

Saturday is the day the tension gets almost unbearable — not because a Giant chokes up or is unable to think, but the right kind of tension, which is released only when you pop someone. The current practice is that the Giants all sleep in town the night before a home game, and of course they are together in their hotel on the road. In New York the Giants have been staying at a hotel on the West Side. There is a curfew and a bed check. By bringing everyone together the night before a game, Allie and the staff believe they can sharpen the mental condition of the men and significantly build morale.

There are no speaking dates accepted by anyone after Wednesday of game week, and the reason is obvious. Off the field, during the week, there is a blackboard discussion every day, usually right before the practice session. Allie is fond of saying that he never wants a team that leaves its games on the practice field during the week. But you'd be surprised how many coaches there were in the past — pro and college — who worked so much on the same repetitious maneuvers that the players simply rebelled. They were *tired* when the big money was on the line. There is too much expensive material involved to treat a professional team like this. And, personally, I think it is one of the best qualities of a pro: he's ready to use his equipment whenever he

25

has to, but he knows when to turn it off, too. Morale in any given week of the season can be a very delicate quality, and a skillful blending of hard work and intelligent change of pace can do more to heighten a team, bringing it to a peak, than rock-hard and repetitious workouts.

Sunday is a day of rest for millions of Americans, but it's the day the world stands still as far as the Giants are concerned. After a midmorning meal (juice and a small steak for most players) the squad usually arrives at the stadium about noon for the 2:05 kickoff. In the locker room, Allie Sherman is with his quarterbacks right from the start. Andy Robustelli is deeply involved with the defense, going over sample situations, perhaps tossing hypothetical problems at his men, seeing how they respond, how well they have got the game defense in mind. One mental mistake, in a rotation or a special defense, for example, and six points are easily the result — for the wrong team. Ken Kavanaugh is with the offensive ends, reviewing their pass patterns, their blocking assignments. Ken is also the spotter on the phone upstairs as soon as the game starts.

The Giants, as most clubs do, now use a Polaroid camera. It is manned by Wel Mara. The photos are dropped to the bench in the famous weighted sock, for a permanent and instant record of what is going on, showing the team how to capitalize when an opportunity next presents itself.

The play charts are also kept most religiously. The whole sequence and pattern of both offense and defense are carefully charted for the Giants as well as the opposition. Frequencies — by field position or specific game situation — are analyzed. What does the opposing quarterback do on second down and two yards, in long yardage situations, when deep in his own territory, etc.?

Of course, at half-time, the emotional appeal that Knute Rockne made famous ("Win one for the Gipper") is most outdated. This precious period is a time for careful discussion and planning, trying to adjust to the opponent's new defense, if he's sprung one, throwing out some basic plays in the game plan that are not working, substituting others, refining as quickly as possible in this short time.

The week officially ends as the final gun sounds, but it doesn't really, as everyone knows. The post-mortems, the might-have-beens are endless. But the mark of a pro is to learn from his mistakes. Just as Y. A. Tittle leaves the field after a successful touchdown drive recounting the plays that got him there, so does he start to replay every series of downs that meant victory or defeat that day.

There might be some beer consumed, some slight socializing on Sunday night. Parties are planned, people come around for autographs, old friends drop by. But this is expected — actually it's the due of everyone who earned it by hard play. But the week that was has gone all too swiftly, and the next Sunday looms big and strong ahead. There is much introspection on the part of the Giants — there must be for them to stay at the top as they have. The fruits are sweet and the defeats bitter, but the circulation of blood, bringing with it old or new aches and pains, comes on too quickly and too inevitably to discount. It's a short, violent week, but the next one is even shorter.

What is actually done out on that field can be easily seen in Dan Rubin's excellent photographs. For example, a double dive by the two deep backs can be entirely tactical, to prepare for some other action far across the field.

There is, in other words, an iceberg quality to this brand of analysis, for seven-eighths of the evident reality is hidden from view. What each man, at each position, is taught to do, what he must perform, is prepared with surgical precision before Dan's pictures can ever be taken. It all starts in training camp months ahead of the kickoff — but the payoff is *how* it's done in the stadium. Before, during, and after the game there are many hidden elements — as with an iceberg — which are crucial to the support of this performance in action. Now let's get out there and take that view, literally from the top.

BEFORE
THE GAME

THERE IS NOTHING more thrilling for many people than to complete that long walk up the ramp of Yankee Stadium and to emerge overlooking that sparkling panorama of green turf opening up before them. The streaming flags, the noises, the smells, the various stimulations are tremendous. But while all this excitement is building among the fans, there is a more prosaic but extremely important ritual taking place on the field.

The Giants are aware of the color, of the tension which is building up around them, but they are down on that mani-

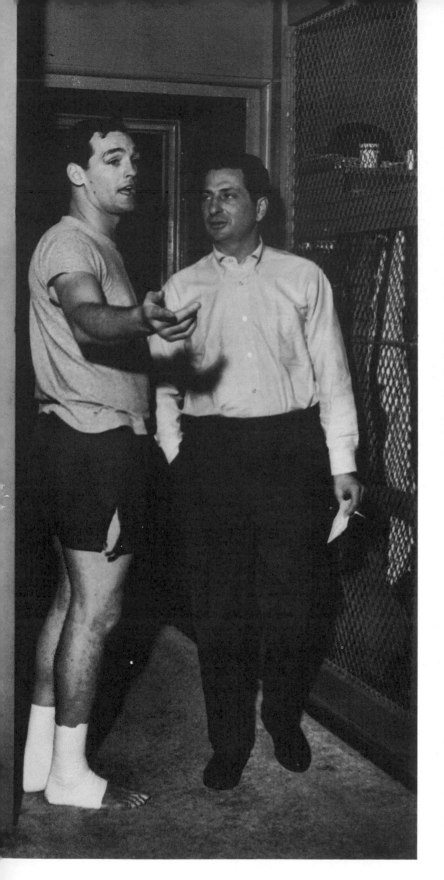

cured piece of land to do a job — and every second counts.

When the team takes the field before a game, there are the many stretching drills, the group and individual exercises that have to be done. The two quarterbacks are at opposite sides of the field, some plays are being run for timing and execution, especially for the halfbacks and the fullbacks. (And often these formations, as academic as they might be, or as diverting, are carefully *watched* by the opposing coach for any hint of what might be coming.)

There is some acting going on now, of course. Webster may be invariably cut-

31

ting back on a certain play, Gifford may be running a certain pattern almost too often to be real, Tittle may be throwing the ball to a certain spot as if he were hypnotized, and so on. The tone again is functional. Every move should be making sense, should be working, however minutely, into the game plan that has been carefully shaped all during the previous week.

Many people have asked me about the "popping" that the Giant linemen engage

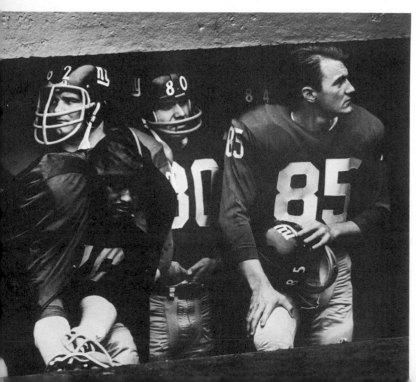

in before a game. There is a reason for this strange activity, too. The men are getting used to their offensive moves, their thrust, their movement off the ball. But perhaps more importantly, they are releasing that awful excitement that has been building all week. Defensive linemen will practice rushing their favorite passer, Y. A. Tittle, defensive backs will

cover receivers as Y. A. tries to hit them down and in, down and out. It all is as close to game situations as possible.

And not a little attention is paid, as all of this action is going on, to the toss of the coin between the opposing captains and the officials. The fans rarely notice this, but you can bet the players and coaches are aware of it. The turn of many a game, the successful momentum a winning team has built, is due to having first crack at the ball. The other toss, the one re-enacted before the television cameras and fans, is a real fix, and this is the only one that we all agree to. The toss is simulated here, but the damage — or the opportunity, depending on your point of view — has already been done.

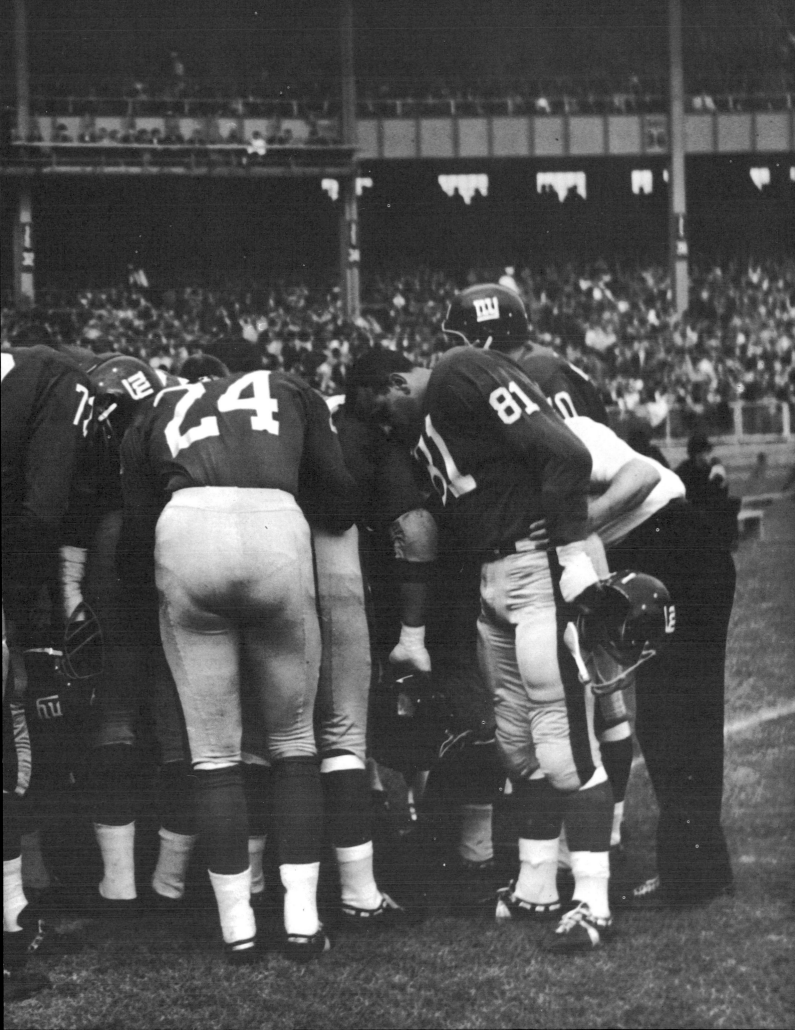

HOW THE GAME
IS PLAYED

YOU WILL GET more out of every game if you know the requirements of each position. I will try to tell you right here some things that I've learned over the years, from playing with the Giants and from years spent since as a scout and a commentator for radio station WNEW.

I don't remember exactly when it all began — this solid sophistication that so many fans now have. Ever since that big 47-7 game with the Bears in 1956, or since the shift from the lamented Polo Grounds to Yankee Stadium, I've seen a growing knowledge on the part of many people. They want the inside story of the game.

When I was sitting near the end zone as a scout for the Giants, busily talking into my little telephone, I could always hear various shouts of suggestion — and they would often be right. Every man is now an analyst — and more power to him. Of course TV has helped bring this about. And the trend is certainly not confined to the male members of our population. Even some women are more aware, more "hip" than ever before. They have to be. They wouldn't be talked to for a whole afternoon otherwise. Our female friends can also be pretty bloodthirsty.

OFFENSE

Let's start with the offensive part of the game: offense is *taught;* defense is *instinct.* The offensive man in professional football must be exceptionally quick,

must be very good at anticipating and adjusting to the defensive patterns that are taking shape in front of him. The offensive man must beat all comers for those first two steps. You've probably heard of 260-pound guards who could outrun a halfback for the first ten yards. Well, it's true. Jack Stroud is extremely difficult to beat in a short race. Look at the films of the 1963 Cleveland–New York game in Cleveland for that. Jack was leading through weak side holes all through the game. Over-all, offense — the Giant offense or any other in the National Football League — works on the unit philosophy. That is, its natural pattern is so well taught and so often repeated that the offensive lineman or back, after a surprisingly short time in the League, will be doing things that he really does not have to think about first. He has been taught, of course, and he is not acting from raw instinct, but his actions are so preordained that he might as well try to change the color of his eyes as to *not* know his basic assignment each time. There are times when the assignment is perfectly accomplished, to quote another Shermanism, and times when it's not. But the basic pattern is ingrained, if the man is to stick for any length of time at all.

As I indicated, the Giants work on the unit philosophy. George Orwell had a name for it: "Group Think," and this term could be applied to the Giants. For example, each tackle and guard will know every play for his position, both left and right. But being in the middle doesn't let the cen-

ter get off with being a little dense. He is actually the brains of the offensive line — he must know more than anyone else up front about blocking patterns, the adjustments to the quarterback's automatic calls (which we'll cover soon), the up-front field generalship that has made Greg Larson and Ray Wietecha so valuable to the Giants over the years.

Any competent physicist knows that a given action produces a given reaction. The Giants know the same thing — only more so. To put it simply: when they forget this basic law, they get a fat lip. The key, in the current New York coaching philosophy, is to establish an offensive *frequency*, a pattern that gives confidence and drive to any sequence of plays.

The Giants have a breakdown on any given situation. Y. A. Tittle has a frequency, a strong belief in a definite play at a certain time in a certain spot on the field. The defensive players he's facing know it; he knows that they know, but he still goes to his strength. Nothing can

demoralize a team faster than to set for Y. A., at second down and two to go, on his own 40-yard line, for instance, knowing full well that he likes to gamble in this kind of a situation. He'll still go for the long one, and when he gets it, the jaws of the biggest guys in that front line drop a foot. You just can't calculate the effect of going with your strength to another's strength — and winning. The challenge is issued and met, and I've seen many a game change drastically after that one crucial play, often in the first quarter.

Bobby Layne had a frequency too. The defense knew his pet plays, but he'd use them anyway. Tittle is especially effective at this, I think, because he will not be forced into what might sound like a contradictory term, "a defensive-offensive position." In other words, he will run the offense the way *he* wants to, and will not necessarily change because of certain defensive weaknesses his coaches and spotters might be constantly thinking of. Also, as Y. A. is quick to point out, the coach, no matter who he is and how good he can be, is not out there, the quarterback is.

The offense must *establish* authority early. That's why you might see Tittle using several running plays quite early in the game, almost always on the first series of downs. This maneuver lets the offensive linemen pop their individual opponents first (and it gets pretty individual up there). The offensive man knows where he is going, and, of course, the defensive man does not. There is a great

40

advantage in this, under the best playing conditions — and especially on wet fields.

The offense must keep the ball; it must score. The great success of the Green Bay Packers over the last few years has been largely due to ball control. The Packers, under the splendid guidance of Vince Lombardi, make very few mistakes on offense, thus not giving their opponents a chance to get the football. As one story goes, Andy Robustelli said to Kyle Rote several years ago, after Andy's defensive squad had scored on an intercepted pass, "Why don't you just try to hold them for a while, Kyle," patting the grimacing Rote on the back and heading for a deserved rest.

People often ask me if there are any special qualifications to play offense. Why does a big, particularly draftable lineman from the Big Ten fail to make the Giants, and a slow but determined, and perhaps undersized, tight end from East Orange Teachers College, to pick a name out of a hat, come through in fine style? There are no set answers, but, the simplest one seems to be explosiveness. Some have got it . . . and you know the rest.

This quality is easy to watch for; it's not so easy to find. For want of a better word, it's that first pop that sets the defensive lineman in his own shade, that fantastic start that shoots a back through the line before the opposing linemen know who to start blaming, in order to protect themselves from Tuesday's Candid Camera.

Added to this explosiveness is the cadence that a good offensive man must set for himself. He doesn't cheat; he just rockets out of that crouch as if he'd been taking lessons from John Glenn. Underneath this philosophy, a conscious one, is the basic adage of "Bury the Man." Explosiveness, timing, cadence — all add up to "the Pop."

Underlying the whole theory of offensive football today is the automatic. No other term seems to get tossed around the stadium more than this one. In the old days, and they weren't too long ago, one play was called against a basic defense, and if the defense stayed the same or if it lined up on its head, the offense would go through with the original call. Well, maybe it wasn't quite that unimaginative, but nothing in the past has quite equaled the flexibility and the variations that the average professional team must now use to keep its momentum and its authority established. Past years saw defenses setting themselves for power plays. Then along came Paul Brown and his Browns, and the whole concept changed. We'll cover this in detail a little later.

Some teams, including the Giants, might use a specific number to signal an automatic, or audible. Others might go for a hot color — red is an obvious one. The opposite might be true: blue, as any good interior decorator knows, is of the cool palate of colors, and might be exactly the key color for that big touchdown play.

No matter what the scheme is, the

automatic has to be used whenever a defense is so set that it can be taken advantage of, or when it will cripple the already determined play.

My experience has been that about three automatics — a dive, a pass play, and a sweep, for instance, will be practiced and sharpened for a particular game. You can get too fancy with this sort of thing, so the list of automatics is limited, as is the number of basic plays.

The myth that many fans believe, that any NFL team has an intricately complex and varied number of super plays that might number five hundred is just not true, because it's not practical. The Giants might easily go into a championship game (and have) with about eight basic running plays to either right or left, with any numbers of passing *variations* out of relatively simple basic pass action. Incidentally, the Giants quarterback on automatic or regular calls is careful to note from time to time the exact position that each defensive back has been assigned. For example, each corner man is usually the strongest on pass defense. The strong-side safety is next, and the weak-side safety is thought generally to be the most vulnerable.

We will get into a position-by-position analysis shortly, but in general terms different positions carry a list of crucial qualifications in today's NFL competition.

Guards are the most able and skilled linemen in the offensive line. They must be able to do more things — pulling for interference, "folding" or circling behind the offensive line for a crucial block, and dropping back on that most important pass-blocking assignment. Tackles must be bulls — big, strong, fast. A 240-pound rookie tackle is going to meet bad news, most of the time, in this game. He will just be too small. Ends obviously differ in the current pro setup. The tight and the split are brothers under the skin (good pass receivers and fakers), but their jobs differ greatly. We will show exactly how, in detail, a little later. Centers, regardless of college grade-point average, must be the smartest men in the offensive line. They must call the offensive line blocking, know everyone's job, be exceptional blockers for both passes and runs, and have the aim and control of a Sandy Koufax — while they have their heads between their legs. In addition, they must anticipate the best rabbit punch in the world falling on their bloody but unbowed skulls.

Offensive backs are a breed apart. And we'll soon see why. Above all, offense must be frenzy and desire, sure, but it's still basically skill and deception. As in boxing, where the good counterpuncher can give fits to the slugger, so can the good offensive man move around and through the hulk he's facing across the line. In order to do this, he must have numerous pieces of impressive mental and physical equipment. Here's a position-by-position analysis of both linemen and backs, as they now most frequently operate in the NFL.

TIGHT END

This crucial position calls loudly for a superlative blocker. As Vince Lombardi has so often said, he has the equivalent of twelve men on the field when he has his tight end Ron Kramer in there, because Kramer can be counted on to take out a man by himself — freeing a lineman for other important blocking assignments.

The tight end must have good speed short; that is, he must be able to grab the look in or other short pass. He must have the deceptiveness that is so necessary to break him loose from linebackers, and

JOE WALTON, 80

he has to be a good analyst — of all three linebackers and their weaknesses, in addition to the deep defenders, who must be outthought during any game under the most varied conditions. He must be a downfield blocker who can block up front first, then move on to pick up an elusive and hard-running defensive back. He really is a combination of a beautiful blocking tackle and a flashy pass receiver who can run all his own patterns superlatively, while spotting all of the weaknesses of both the defensive line and backfield. As if these superhuman responsibilities weren't enough, he must be able to take that constant, draining contact up front. Don't forget that this man is con-

stantly knocking heads with the biggest defensive men on the field. Kramer is probably the best example of the man with all the marbles, and then comes Mike Ditka of the Chicago Bears; but Giants Joe Walton and Aaron Thomas, though without the great physical equipment of a Kramer, meet all the qualifications listed above, and the Giants have got the maximum from their potential.

SPLIT END

Many college halfbacks who are great pass catchers with above-average speed find themselves assigned to this spot. The importance of elusiveness and faking ability is obvious. This is a money, a glory,

44

position, but one with great responsibility. The average fan may see this man go down and out to catch the big payoff pitch, but he knows, too, that it didn't come about easily. This position calls for real endurance. The ability to go down, very deep, as a decoy, running the defensive back out of the play for someone else coming across the field short is just one tiring and taxing maneuver that must be constantly repeated. Then, on that fourth play, for example, the pressure is on to catch the big one. Maybe the defensive back is dropping off just a step now — after several dry runs. This calls for maximum effort and superlative conditioning.

Having great hands here is a real must. Getting loose is meaningless if the ball won't stick. Del Shofner is most accomplished at making this position as important as it is in the Giants' offense. Del must be able to come back to the huddle and tell Tittle that he can beat his man — and then do it. The big play is his — but the big drop can be very easily seen from every seat in the stands.

Last of all, the split end must run his patterns accurately and well. If the play calls for down twelve yards and out, that has to be done to the last blade of grass.

DEL SHOFNER, 85

47

There is no room in professional football for vagueness, to be sure, and at no other place is accuracy more necessary.

FLANKER BACK

This man's duties and responsibilities are quite similar to those of the split end. In fact, on the Giants and on most NFL teams, you will find these two interchanging. The flanker back must be fast and a sure pass catcher. In a rather special way, he must be one of the most perceptive men on the squad. In many a key game, a defensive tip, a slight weakness will be picked up by this man. For example, he might see a defensive back take a fake that could be fatal for him. The flanker will return quickly and report to his quarterback. And often it only takes one such report to tip the scales in a game. Frank Gifford is especially adept at doing

48

49

this. Around the league, Frank is known and feared for this uncanny ability to spot a giveaway that can tear apart an otherwise airtight defense. The flanker back has to be a contributor, the man who can come up with the big play at the most opportune time.

Again, let's take Gifford as an example. Last December in Yankee Stadium things could have gone much differently in the big game against Pittsburgh. The Steelers were getting tougher and tougher, and time was running out. Then Gifford made that miraculous shoestring grab of Tittle's pass that kept an important drive going and helped to prevent the Steelers from getting the ball and stalling the Giants momentum. Many experienced observers thought Frank made the biggest contribution of the season during that one play.

The flanker is an astute actor and decoy, too. He must be able to cut at the very best spot, to take a defensive man in when the pass is going to an end down and out, or to a swing man coming around to where that halfback who's going back with the flanker would normally be.

FRANK GIFFORD, 16

50

JACK STROUD, 66

TACKLE

Size is a basic requirement here. And the price of bigness keeps going up. I think nowadays that this minimum standard could be put on tackles in the NFL: 6 feet 5 inches tall and 260 pounds. Who knows, in a few years, it may go to 300. By the same token, height helps a lot in this position. This is most noticeable in pass blocking. A tall *and* heavy tackle can block a lot of charging bodies and give that valuable passer a split second more time to get the ball off. When you're working within a normal firing time of only four seconds, every half-second counts.

A good tackle has excellent balance.

52

From his compact stance, he must be able, as in the Giants offense, to pull for wide plays or drop back for pass protection. He must be exceptionally quick

off the ball, and it is quite important that he be consistent. In fact, it's critical. A "pointing" tackle can give away more plays than almost anyone else on the field. His eyes, even his shoulders, his toes — all have to work in unison, often acting in the best dramatic fashion, to prevent the defense from knowing the direction of the play. Rosey Brown fills my bill of particulars for this spot, and, of course, Jim Parker at Baltimore, who is probably the best in the league.

ROSEY BROWN, 79

GUARD

All of the moves for this position are covered by those listed for the tackle — and then there are some more. For example, the guard must be able to pull and lead interference almost as quickly as a halfback can reach his hole. He must be a very good pass protector, and one of the strongest blockers on the run — for he may be blocking the most powerful defensive man — the tackle opposite him. The guard often has to pop and then get out to the flank fast — for screens. His first two steps are crucial for him, and his success often makes or breaks the reputation of the running backs behind him. Witness the Giants' Darrell Dess and the Packers' Jerry Kramer as superior operators in this department.

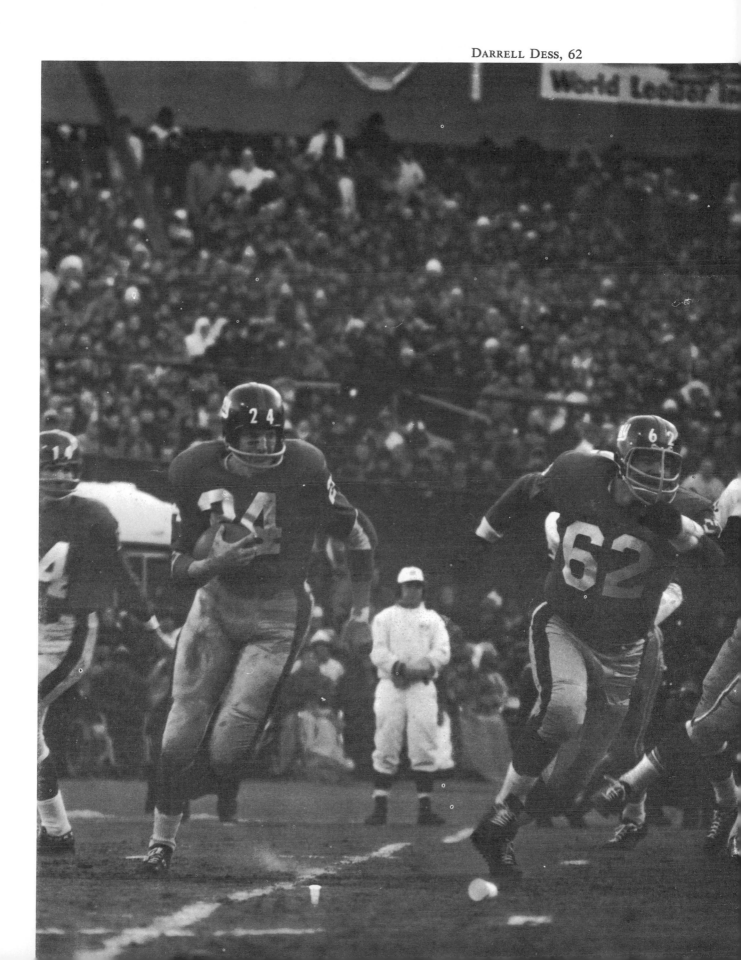

BOOKIE BOLIN, 63

CENTER

As I said earlier, this man must have a superior mind. He calls blocking assignments, passes back for extra points and punts, and picks up any red-dog and blitz maneuvers of the defense. He also has to be a good feinter and must help form the cup that the pro quarterback steps up into after he has taken his allot-

GREG LARSON, 53

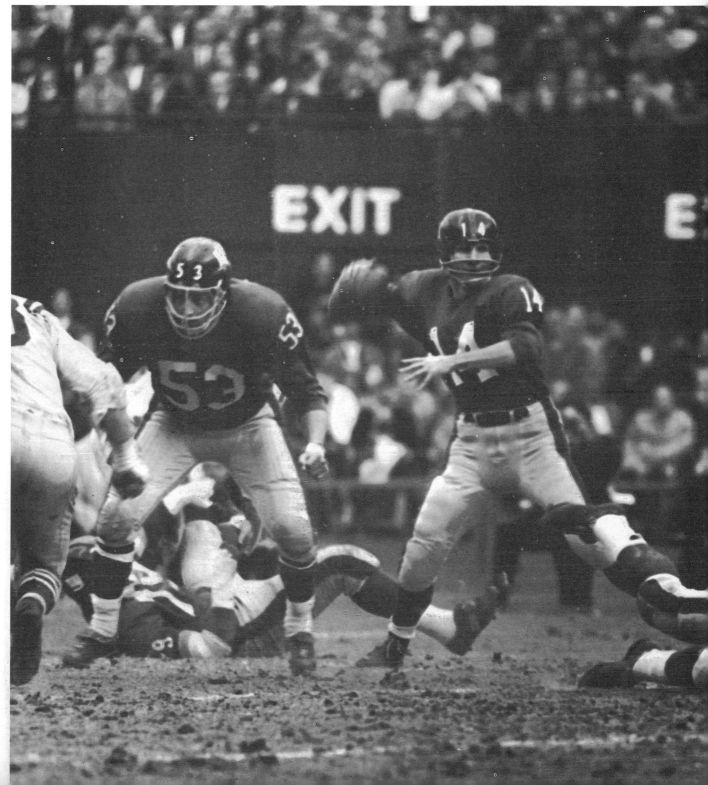

ted steps back from the line. The code of the center is a simple one: his initial pop must be terrific, or the offense is in trou- ble. Greg Larson, and before him the great Ray Wietecha, are examples of most valuable men.

ALEX WEBSTER, 29

FULLBACK

Size is a real asset here, of course, but great explosiveness is probably more important. The fullback must know his holes

61

extremely well. He can be most valuable, as Jimmy Brown is, if he can hit and slide, keeping his balance after that initial shock, blasting into the secondary and eventual daylight. The fullback is invaluable if he has this running balance — and if he can be a good blocker, too. Paul Hornung and Jim Taylor help each other a great deal because the defense cannot depend on one of them not being murderous while his mate is carrying the ball. In other words, if Hornung is going off

62

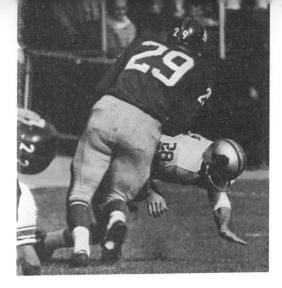

tackle, Taylor will be leading the crunching for him. This is a great morale factor: if one running back knows his associate is beating his brains out, he'll do the same thing himself. But it's amazing how often this isn't done.

The fullback must have sure hands in

PHIL KING, 24

order to catch the flare pass, and great lateral mobility to run the sweep. He must be quick to diagnose a red dog that will change his running pattern. Last of all, he must be durable, as tough and long-lasting as any man on the offensive platoon.

HALFBACK

This man must have balance equal to that of the fullback, and must be just as good a blocker. In addition, he must be quick outside (which might not be the

JOE MORRISON, 40

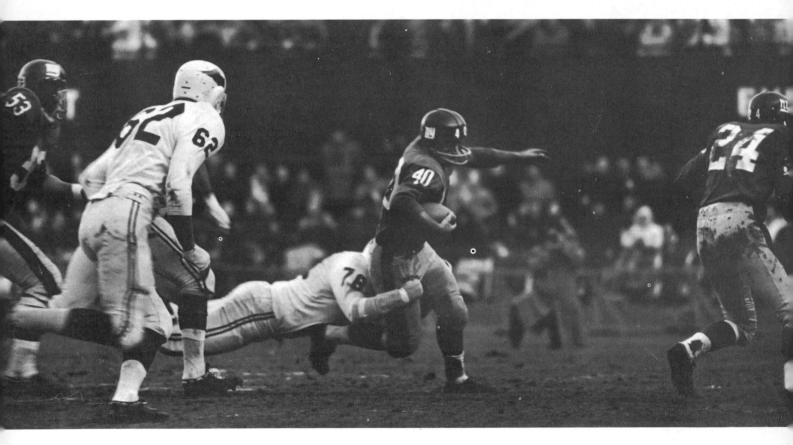

64

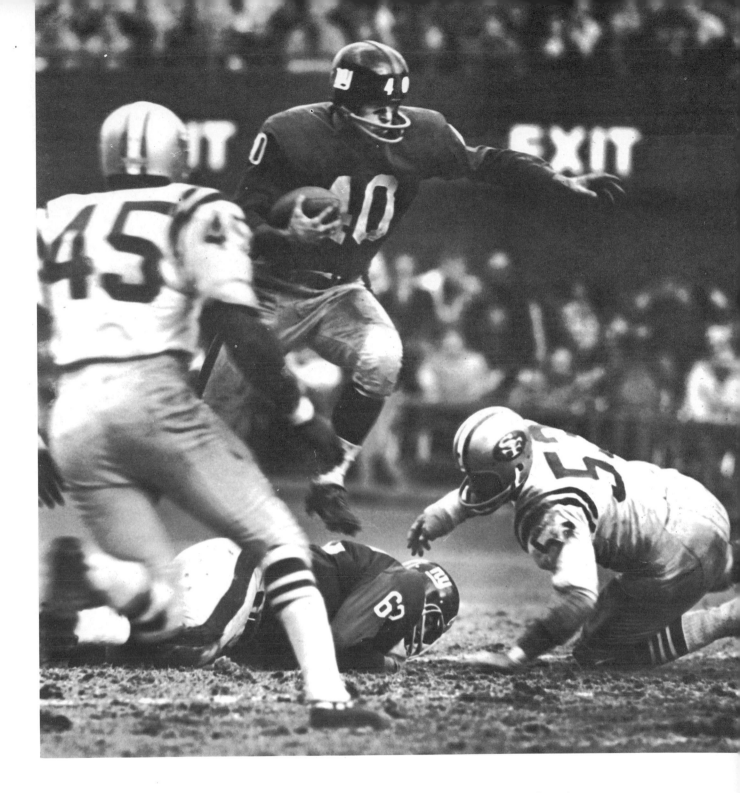

case with the fullback, Jimmy Brown excluded), and he must especially be good at the cutback, inside. His blocking on pass protection, like the fullback's, must be superb, and his hands sure for the safety-valve pass, the down and in, and the down and out. He must know every phase of all pass patterns, and he must

run them perfectly, in order to mesh with the flanker back and the split end. Halfbacks can no longer be slight and slippery types. They are in a heavy-duty role, one that demands both durability and finesse.

QUARTERBACK

The maestro must be a take-charge guy. He will listen in the huddle (and should), but he will never let the team direct him. He leads and marshals them in everything they do. Of course, in this league, at this time, his passing must be superb. He must

Y. A. TITTLE, 14

have great poise and courage, for he fully realizes the moment he releases the ball, a thousand-plus pounds of frenzy are going to hit him. And believe it or not, he gets hit, fairly, on almost every play. He's out there to be hit, and he knows — and expects — that those up-front defensive men are going to make sure he's on his back whenever they can.

The quarterback must be able to spot defensive weaknesses immediately and take advantage of them. He is a dedicated

man, and I mean this sincerely. He spends more time thinking and planning than any other player on the squad. His job is never easy, never the same from one minute to the next. He must be able to go

for a first down on a rollout — and hope that his coach's heart will take the unnatural strain of seeing all that talent and leadership possibly being destroyed. He must, above all, be brisk and intelligent out there. He must adjust quickly, capitalize and direct. His execution must be perfect, and he must know exactly what every man is doing on every play.

His bread-and-butter pass, it seems to me, is the down and out. He must know exactly when to throw the ball away on this kind of play, or he will be the only tackler who can bar the door on thieving halfbacks like Dick Lynch, who pray, who make novenas, that they'll catch a weary quarterback giving a football away.

The quarterback must move back from the scrimmage extremely fast, and then have the courage and discipline to move *up* into the cup his offensive linemen have formed for him in the teeth of the onrushing defensive men. So many good

college quarterbacks never seem to work into this cup strategy. They are used to running to the side and then passing, often suicidal in the NFL. The QB is the nerve center of the entire team. His perception and skill may make the afternoon uncomplicated bliss, or a living hell. It helps for him to be tall, also.

He must have the manual dexterity of a Las Vegas blackjack dealer and the basic honesty of a Benedictine monk. In essence, he is Everyman to his team. And if he's good, he's often a god. Cases in point: Otto Graham, Y. A. Tittle, Bobby Layne. As Allie said once, with a trace of seriousness: "When Tittle retires, so do I."

Offense is a game of constant concentration and team effort even when one man may not be directly involved in the immediate action area most noticeable to the average fan. Again our iceberg metaphor. Offense is relentless but entirely

flexible. A good coach builds to fit his material and has no rigid preconceptions of making his manpower conform to his vision of the perfect offense, one that just has to work under any circumstances. These offensive theories — and these coaches — are no longer around. They met defenses that wouldn't play fair . . . they moved around the field.

DEFENSE

As an old defensive man, let me make one simple, immodest statement: the best men are always put on this squad. It is inevitable. Seriously, many coaches will agree: the men with the best natural equipment are often the best qualified to play defense in pro football, because, as I've stated before, the defensive side of the game is instinct, and a great many of the natural moves that a defensive man makes cannot be taught — at least not very quickly. And professional football, being a most competitive business, cannot take time to train men for the future, as a sales manager might be able to go along for a while with a less than perfectly producing salesman. The defense must produce — fast.

The defense is paid, frankly, to punish the offense. It must anticipate the entire rationale of the opposing quarterback and beat him at his own game. It is not easy to do, believe me, but a good defensive man must know more about his offensive opponent than the offense knows about the defense.

The defense does enjoy a certain advantage, though. Blocking is not a natural move, it must be learned, and the defensive man in his rush can use his natural instincts against the blocker. He can also use his hands.

The areas of responsibility on defense are also more defined than on offense. Don't get me wrong: the defensive game is for real thinking men. First, the up-front linemen have *many* areas of responsibility. They must pressure the passer at all times, contain or strip each running play, close off the middle, handle traps and fold blocks. Above all, they must get that ball so the offense can score. Oddly enough, as some ingenious defensive man has reported, there are more ways for the defense to score than there are for the offense. This is a slight bonus for the bruises and aches that a good defensive man must suffer.

There are many reasons for the increased sophistication of today's defensive maneuvers. One is the tremendous ability of modern passers to score against you from virtually any spot on the field. A decent amount of time given to any accomplished passer can mean disaster for even the best defense. As a result, there is a strong emphasis today on the specialized defense, the flexible unit that can move to any spot, at any time, to close off a threat that might be entirely new to the game plan.

There are certain characteristics that a defensive coach like Andy Robustelli constantly tries to instill into his team:

75

control, leverage, balance, awareness, and so on. Variations on variations are the rule, and the rigid man ends up last every time. Using the typical 4-3-4 defense, let's look, as we did on offense, at the basic qualities that make a defensive man.

END

He must be the bull of the defense. Height is a real asset in rushing the passer, much more so than with the interior men of the front four. This man must be a good faker, which may sound surprising, because of his defensive position. However, like Robustelli, this guy must be able to give a head and shoulder fake outside before going inside, in order to evade that block-

JIM KATCAVAGE, 75

ing lineman or back. The end must also have raw speed — there's no other way to put it. Quickness, surely, but real speed, too — to protect the outside, of course. Special dangers of this position are the trap and the screen, especially if the man is really good at his position; more effort will be made to run around a good man here than over him. The end must show excellent pursuit and determination, perhaps more than anyone else on the defensive team. The first pop here is sometimes child's play compared to the bruising that comes next. Last of all, the end must be able to strip interference in order to make the tackle possible for the corner line-

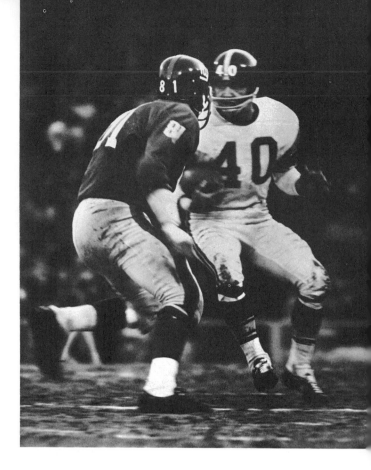

ANDY ROBUSTELLI, 81

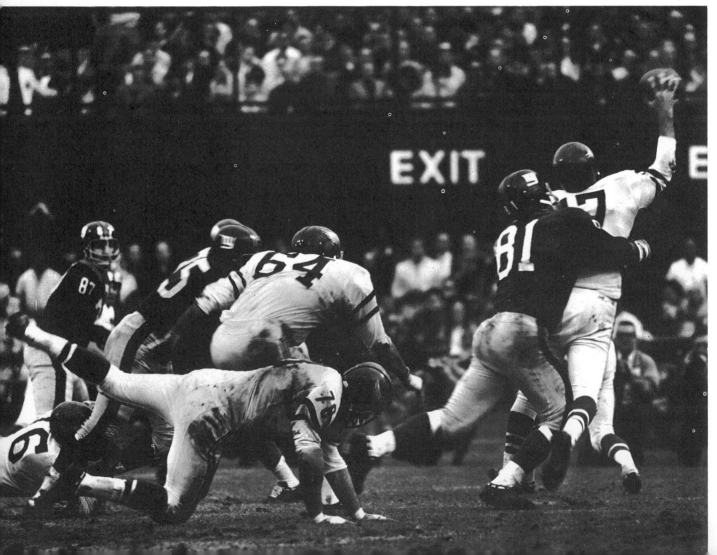

JOHN LoVETERE, 76

backer or the halfback or the safety who is coming up. Excellent operator at this spot: Jim Katcavage.

TACKLE

This interior man must have tremendous power at point of impact. He should be able to take more punishment than anyone else, for a sustained period of time — and come back for more. Here, lack of height is often an asset because a smaller target is offered to the blocker. For example, a short-legged man can be very difficult to raise up with a trap block. This interior defensive man can't ever raise up and do the job right. The tackle must be strong, able to handle the dive, react to the outside if he has to, rush the passer with the greatest abandon, and above all, keep his balance. He must protect the middle and use his hands well

TOM SCOTT, 82

to destroy the slashing pattern on the typical power play inside. First-rate example: John LoVetere.

CORNER LINEBACKER

Besides being large, this man must be exceptionally quick. He must be able to cover a swing man deep, be able to fight off blockers as though he owned them, and be mean enough to handle tight ends like Mike Ditka. This man must rush the passer, but still be deft enough to recover and tackle surely if the quarterback gets

82

BILL WINTER, 31

83

outside him. A corner linebacker should be really good at the red dog. He must be an above-average tackler, for many of his tackles are loners, and the damage is severe if he misses. The strong-side man has the most pressure put on him, while the weak-side man must be flexible and good at both the red dog and storm.

JERRY HILLEBRAND, 87

MIDDLE LINEBACKER

This defensive team leader should be the hardest man on the field to knock down. His responsibilities are the greatest — and he must prove equal to them by making more tackles than any other man in the game. The MLB must be able to cover offensive fullbacks deep, and also be able to move into the line if necessary. A tre-

86

mendous range of activity — and excellence — is expected here. As defensive spark plug, this position calls for great analytical ability, the vision and the sense to read plays, and to communicate this knowledge to all the other defensive men. He is constantly keying on the opposition's fullback or on a guard for any advantage he can get.

SAM HUFF, 70

Dick Lynch, 22

ERICH BARNES, 49

HALFBACK

This rangy fellow should be the best all-around back on the defensive team. He must be able to do as well on man-to-man coverage as he does on zone. The corner man must be a keen student of the offensive pattern that the opposing quarter-back has set up. What, for example, does the Steeler's Ed Brown like to do when he's in trouble? What play will Bart Starr call if he thinks you're all set for Taylor up the middle? He also keys on every play, watching the tight end or the strong-

side guard for any indication of where the play is going. This position takes an exceptional football player. He must be the deadliest of solitary tacklers, while being quick and savvy enough to intercept his share of passes, both in the flat and deep. The halfback should make the fewest mental errors of anyone on the defensive platoon. An error for him often results in a TD. In the strong-side position he has much pressure put on him during sweeps, down and in and down and out

91

pass patterns. The weak-side corner back must be able to cover the fast split end all by himself.

STRONG-SIDE SAFETY

This man must know exactly how far he can go on every play. He must have more

than a little of the gambler in him, and he must have great natural anticipation. His technique is more definite than the weak-side safety. For instance, he often keys on the tight end and most of the time is closer to the line than the weak-side safety. This position is particularly vul-

92

nerable to the play-action pass, where one false move, one careless commitment, can mean disaster.

WEAK-SIDE SAFETY

This man has the largest over-all area to cover on the field. Speed here is especially valuable. He must be able to help on the inside run as well as drop quickly to cover the deep or swing man. Often a free-floating operator, this man must be able to tackle in the open, for he is often the deepest man and the last chance to bar the door to six points.

We hear a good bit of talk nowadays about the differences between zone and man-to-man pass defense. The zone is played by many teams, and is most effec-

DICK PESONEN, 25

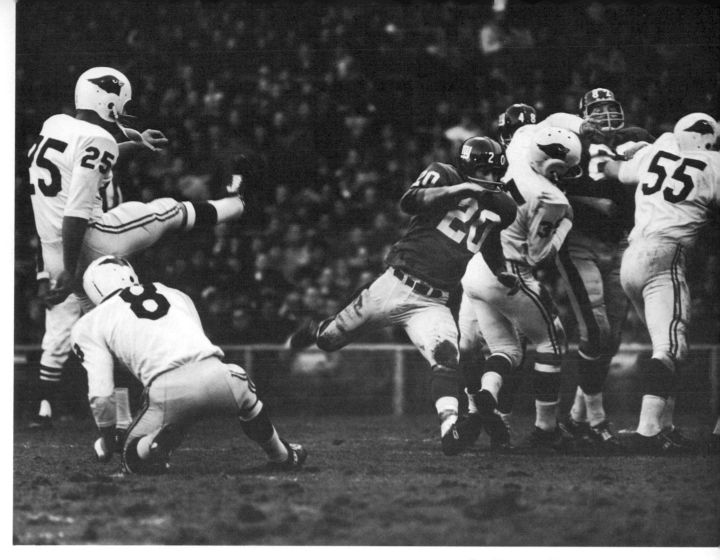

JIM PATTON, 20

tive. But it can be picked to pieces by the right quarterback. Again, see the films of last season's New York-Cleveland game at Cleveland. Man-to-man coverage is the toughest, demands the most from the defensive personnel, and puts a terrible burden on the defensive lineman, who *must* hurry the passer.

The defense is constantly trying to keep the offense from doing its best. The modern 4-3-4 came into being largely because of the fantastic ability of the old Cleveland Browns to make a defense look bad. With great ends, a great blocking and running fullback, and a phenomenal quarterback, the Browns, coached by Paul Brown, moved with awesome finesse over almost everyone they met. As a result, the late Steve Owen devised the famous umbrella defense, which dropped the standard six-man defensive line, to go to at least a version of the 4-3-4 which most pro teams use now. In the umbrella, the 6-1-4, only the two ends need drop off to make a 4-3-4. Greasy Neale of the Philadelphia Eagles experimentcd a great deal with this, paving the way for much of Sherman's philosophy. Paul Brown

ALLAN WEBB, 21

concentrated on a split line, excellent receivers, great passing (with Otto Graham) and most effective punting (Horace Gillom) and field goal kicking (Lou Groza). Against the standard six, the receivers could beat you short; the swing back could wreck you outside; the fullback (Marion Motley) forced you to

protect the middle; and the quarterback, who could do anything, passed, ran, screened, drew, and kept you off balance. So the 4-3-4 was born and almost revolutionized the game. It gave more flair and importance to the defense and made possible the interesting defense-offense challenges just described.

97

THE KICKING GAME

THE KICKOFF

You won't find Tittle or Gifford on the kickoff squad, going down under one of Don Chandler's booming efforts. It's too dangerous courting injury to men like these on this kind of play. The men who are on the kickoff squads have their own

value; kicking off and returning kicks constitute two of the most important (and hazardous) plays in professional football. As a result, there is a great need for special men with special equipment for these jobs.

98

First of all, you must have great speed. The fine job that Mickey Walker has been doing on kickoffs is due largely to his exceptional speed, and to that old intangible — desire. You must have suicidal types on this kind of play. The kickoff play is, to me, one of the most exciting in all of football. I'll never forget one of the most thrilling examples of this. In the early 1950's Buddy Young, the former Illinois great, was playing with the New York Yankees. The Giants had another incomparable, Emlen Tunnell, on their kickoff receiving unit. In one game between the Yankees and the Giants, Young went all the way on one play, and before the excited gallery could sit down, Em ran the ensuing kickoff all the way back for the Giants. You very rarely see one of these back-to-back situations, but when you do it's unforgettable.

The primary responsibility of the suicide squad is to turn the receiver inside. Often the most important cog in this tough machine is the man who has that unpleasant but crucial responsibility of throwing his body into the forming offensive wedge. And this has been a job that Walker, among others, has excelled at over the last few years. The wedge cannot always be anticipated, of course, and there are many variations that each team will use. But many plays have gone all the way when this center alley was cleared for some speedy back.

The talented kickoff man can be worth his weight in green stamps, if not in gold.

In Don Chandler, the Giants have one of the best in the NFL. But because of his very value, other teams point up for him on every kickoff. You have probably watched an opposing lineman push forward immediately after Don has kicked, moving directly for him. This is entirely fair and to be expected. A 260-pound tackle's presence can be bothersome to the most courageous fellow, especially if he knows that a few steps after he has kicked the ball he may be splattered. But there are ways to defend against such carnage, such waste of a valuable man, as far as the Giants are concerned. They have a special man on their kickoff team who guards Chandler, who in turn acts as the final safety valve in case the returning back does shoot the gap of Giants and is in danger of going for long yardage. Sounds quite complicated, I'll admit, but it's simple if you watch the right men — who are watching their men, who are watching, in turn . . . well, you know what I mean.

Although it may not always look that way, there is a well-defined play on every time for both the offense and defense. The key for the kicking team is to get that ball deep in opposing territory — and in bounds. Nothing is quite as offensive to a kickoff lineman as to run to the winds only to get called back and start all over — from five yards behind where he left the last time. Getting the ball high on a kickoff is obviously important. It gives the rushing linemen time to cover, to do their assigned tasks. It is extremely dangerous to kick a blue dart, a screamer, to use a baseball phrase, that someone like Abe Woodson catches about three seconds after the ball has left the kicker's foot. You are in real trouble then, because the defensive team is a very long way from completing, or even really beginning, its defensive responsibilities. If certain lanes are open, they can never be closed in time with a real speedster coming up field.

The kickoff is a glamorous play, and it's most important for the kicker not to add to this excitement with his own generosity. He therefore intends to keep the ball away from the dangerous, the proved, return expert. But he can't be so conscious of this that he will squirt the ball short, which means a big handicap to his defensive brethren, or kick it out of bounds and be penalized.

The most practical kickoff defense is to work by well-defined lanes; that is, to assign each man a vertical segment of the

DON CHANDLER, 34

JERRY HILLEBRAND, 87; CHARLIE KILLETT, 37; LANE HOWELL, 78; LOU KIROUAC, 71; KEN BYERS, 60

playing field. Nothing should go over this man in his lane. The first wave is taking the receiver any way, by any method it can. The outside men are then faced with turning the receiver in, so the two waves form a pincer to trap the ball carrier. He's got his thoughts, too, about evading all of this careful planning, as we'll soon see.

There are also special kickoff plays designed around peculiar game conditions. A typical one is the on-side kick, where the ball has to go ten yards, at which time it becomes free — for anyone to recover. Placing the ball flat, the kicker will squib it, hoping that he's skillful enough to make it go the required yardage and that one of his teammates will recover it. Whenever this situation develops, you'll see two exceptionally fast men, like Erich Barnes and Dick Lynch, on either side of Don Chandler, trying to make use of their great speed to recover the free ball.

Curious as it may sound, a fumbled kickoff can work most effectively *against* the kicking team (rather than the receiving one) if certain conditions are right. For example, the fumbled kick will cause the average lineman to relax a trifle, even if he's most experienced — it's only natural. Then, when he recovers from this lapse, he could well see a streak of opposing lightning coming by him at a rate of speed too great to intercept or alter. I've seen this happen many times on a low, fast kick that might be very difficult to handle. The kicking team will delay just a fraction, enough for the recovering team to seize an opportunity they might not have had before. Over-all, the theme of this most exciting play in football is pursuit and containment. Get down hard and fast, force the play into the squeezing defensive area, and get possession of the ball, if possible.

In recent years, some criticism has been leveled at the Giants for this phase of their otherwise excellent defensive operation. Sherman is constantly working on new methods, new combinations of material, new pursuit plans — all to remedy and improve, for the perfect execution he and the rest of the coaches seek. The cover on a kickoff can be most effective in terms of team morale, so it's worth noting again that nothing can damage the spirit more than a long, deep kickoff that results in minus thirty yards. There you are — rushing onto the field to assume your defensive burden, first and ten on your own 15-yard line.

Just as the kicking team puts fast men in, the receiving team relies on its fastest backs and linemen. Johnny Counts, for example, has been most effective for the Giants because of his great speed. Woodson has been discussed before. His leaping, twisting runs have put San Francisco in more than one advantageous field position early in the game. Even old unemotional linemen will pause to thank those favored backs for making such a break possible.

The low kick is a blessing, of course, because it gives the offense time to form with virtually no opposition. A low screamer can mean trouble, though, because any kickoff within the confines of the playing field is a free ball, and a recovery in the end zone by the onrushing team means a very cheap and very damaging six points — and hell to pay for the receiving team on Tuesday.

Once in a while, I'll be asked about a big lineman returning a kickoff. How

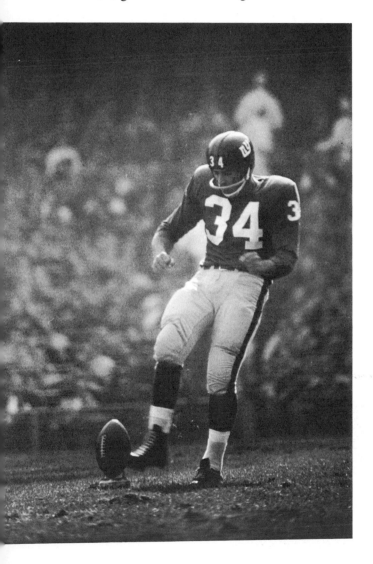

does he feel, what goes through his mind? Usually, he's wondering how to lateral, and to whom. He's been taught to get rid of the ball, then try to set up the original play as the offense begins to form. It's not as unselfish as it might seem, because it's a lot easier to knock somebody off who's coming downfield than to have all eleven after you — especially if you haven't been practicing your cross-over steps and your limp leg action.

The kicking team at kickoff time is a well-oiled and thoroughly briefed special unit that knows that, if it does its job correctly, the whole complexion of any game, right from the start, can be changed in its favor. When they are receiving, the Giants currently use an offensive formation of four men up front, on the 45-yard line, two men at the 30, three more men at the 15, and two deep men at the goal line. As soon as the ball is kicked, each man begins his specific assignment. Yes, there is a Giant to go after the kicking specialist who has just boomed one far downfield.

Each opposing team member, as a matter of fact, is numbered, so that there is no confusion during the action. Each number carries a corresponding Giants number to take him out. The wedge that is immediately formed is the personal escort of the ball carrier. There are variations on the wedge, certain pockets in the defense that are widened and trapped according to the specific play that the Giants have on at a particular time. The "other" deep man, the one who does not receive

103

the ball, becomes the traffic director for the return. The optimum return is for the touchdown, as anyone knows, but the importance of a good, deep return cannot be overemphasized.

PUNTING

In today's brand of professional football, the punting game has regained as important a place as it enjoyed during the early 1930's, for example, in college ball, when players like Frank Carideo could drop a handkerchief on the goal line and hit it regularly from sixty yards away. The emphasis has changed a bit, however. Now the booming punts by most NFL specialists are just as accurate, but they are often even longer than the healthy record set by Carideo and his compatriots. You don't often see a punt returned in the NFL nowadays; , the height of each one is so tremendous that defensive halfbacks have very little chance to do more than signal for a fair catch. The speed of even the biggest linemen appears to have increased so much in recent years that this vital and thrilling element of the game may be going through a decided change.

There are exceptions, and when these occur, the curtain is up on one of the most completely team-action plays in the game. There is slight attention paid, while the game is going on, to that vital area of punt exchanges, the yards-gained or -lost

column, but when everything is finished, the plus or minus position of your team in this department can spell victory or defeat.

Today's punters, Chandler in particular, stand about twelve to fifteen yards behind the center, and they move into the ball with the greatest care for their timing. "One-two-boom" is the familiar phrase around the Giants scene, and this describes the whole affair quite well.

Greg Larson does not snap the ball on an audible signal. He sets himself, looks back, gets Don's position, and then does not look again. He's got his own problems staring him full in the face, and he doesn't want to *not* see what hits him. Because of his unerring aim, his slight jump on the other linemen, and his unusual speed for a man of his size, Larson is almost always the first man downfield on a punt. The rhythm of the entire operation is dependent on the blocking up front, of course. In the line, that initial pop has to be stiff enough to stop the initial charge of the defense. The lane of attack has to be cut off, so the offensive man must be constantly watching for head and shoulder fakes or a defensive "fold" or pulling pattern, where one man will pull the offensive blocker through his lane preparing for a linebacker or other back to shoot the gap. As far as the offensive blocking backs are concerned, two are lined upon the strong side, one man on the weak. For a right-footed kicker,

the formation is strong right — and strong left for a left-footed punter.

One of the main responsibilities for the blockers is to protect their individual lanes; they must never cross over to take an oncoming defensive man who may be shooting. An embarrassing example of this is sometimes brought back to haunt Mickey Walker. He crossed over once, in a burst of enthusiasm, and he got hit in the back by his own punter's effort. A well-launched punt in the chest or in the small of the back can mean smelling salts, and an especially disadvantageous field position — a minus fifty yards or so — the difference between the average Chandler punt (with no run back) and the ball being recovered behind your own line.

Both backs and linemen must be prepared to cover the kick once it is gotten off. The defensive line may immediately fold either right or left, depending on field position, time of game, and the particular formation that has been called. The kicking team, now on defense, must get to the ball carrier fast once he has started to move with the punt. This is the special job of the first man down, who, for the Giants, has consistently been Greg Larson.

The fake punt formation can be important, though its use is now fairly infrequent in the NFL. At the discretion of the punter, this play can be put into action any time — most often when the defense has folded a little too quickly, telling the punter that no rush is on and a special effort is under way to spring the punt receiver for a long return. The punter can either run or pass, of course, and this play has rescued many teams from tough spots.

The defensive man who is lucky enough to block a punt has followed one simple rule: "He has gone to the foot." Otherwise, he won't have the time, frankly; the distance back to the punter, with today's excellent centers, is just too great.

The most pressure on today's punting specialists is put on them in their own end zones, where the distance back from center can be only ten yards, for instance, instead of the normal fifteen. The wet field, the effects of wind — all are adverse factors. But the great effectiveness of the punt today is brought about by the incredible power and skill of the kickers currently in action.

Pro football today, as I've pointed out, uses the fair catch most of the time. But the ball must be caught, you know, or it's entirely free. Just as this deadly sin (dropping a punt) might be thought to be inexcusable, so is any roughing the kicker penalty — in the eyes of most coaches. Not that there isn't some great acting going on out there. I don't think Don Chandler is going to make things rough for Richard Burton this year, but he does do his job well — and Don is sure to show his fragility, especially when the opposing line gets too close.

The longest punter, oddly enough, may

not be of great value to his team, if he is inaccurate. This quality of accuracy has stood more punters in good stead, has assured more of them that they will get their NFL pensions, than any other attribute. As obvious as it is, those boomers that sail long and far over the goal mean the opponents take over the ball on their own 20-yard line. But that squiggly, that miserable but well-directed punt that gasps out finally in the coffin corner can cause many loud curses.

THE FIELD GOAL AND THE POINT AFTER TOUCHDOWN

It was Steve Owen, the Giants' head coach from 1931 to 1953, who did as much to build the field goal as an offensive weapon as anyone else in the history of the game. Steve made the league and his own men play for the field goal in place of the touchdown, taking a sure three points when perhaps a gamble for the TD would mean nothing but frustration and eventual defeat. Steve's theory has borne great fruits for the Giants — and for their toughest opponents over the years. But a perfect field goal cannot even begin without a perfect snap, and that's why an NFL pro at center must be a *real* pro. He knows that he's going to get creamed when that snap goes back, but he must be able to hit the holder of the ball chest-high every time. From there, the ball goes down as if it had eyes. That's why a substitute quarterback is usually picked for this specialized duty. He's got good hands, and he's most familiar with handling a wet — or a dry — ball. And don't think that the man in this position is all steel and ball bearings, either. He's in a most vulnerable spot, fully exposed while a thundering herd charges to get that precious ball, or at least to use up a few of their stationary (and kneeling) opponents in the process.

The kicker cannot even afford to watch the ball coming back to his holder. He watches nothing except the spot where the ball is to be placed. Of course, the timing here is essential, but so also is the blocking up front. The block must be held longer for the field goal than for the point after touchdown, but the motions are basically the same — one-two-kick; only the distance varies. The biggest and most powerful linemen are put in for these two plays. They've got to have the best pops on the team, the best initial thrust, and the most power and speed off the mark.

In field-goal strategy, many times you will see a quarterback going only for position on the field, especially late in the game. He runs a sweep to get good field position, or he runs a dive that will maintain it for the next vital play, the attempt for three points. If you've noticed, more and more NFL games lately have been decided in this very department. The field-goal specialist and the point-after-touchdown man, often the same guy, can be compared to a relief pitcher in baseball, and recent records will bear out how

GLYNN GRIFFING, 15

108

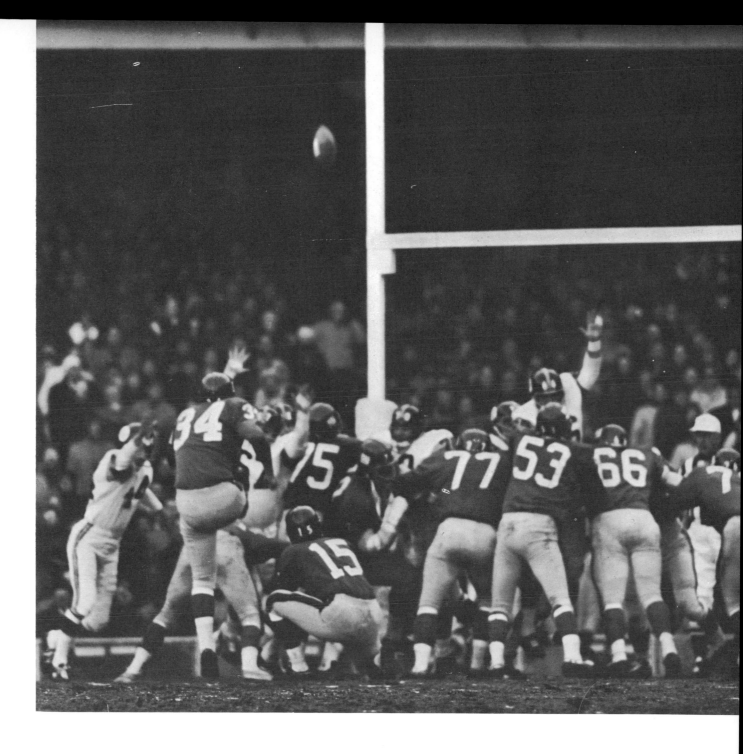

often he leads the NFL in total scoring at the end of a season.

In the last few years, there has been some talk about the point after touchdown becoming so automatic that it ought to be increased in distance or replaced by the Canadian *rouge,* where each punt must be run out of the end zone or a point is scored against the receiving team. Points-after are still blocked, passes from center still go bad, but it does seem that something could be devised to make this phase of the game a little more colorful, unpredictable, and stimulating.

THE SIDELINE

Gone forever are the days when fans, policemen, ice-cream vendors, and the owner's cousin moved easily and freely around the bench of any major profes-sional team. Now it is like a command post for a battle.

There is a definite order to everything on the Giants bench. Defensive men are

seated in one block, under the guidance of Andy Robustelli, while the offensive troops are in another section, under the constant observation of Allie Sherman. Players move on and off quickly, reporting anything they feel may be useful and helpful to their respective coaches. Substitute quarterbacks, in the Giants' case Glynn Griffing, are on the phone to the spotters. Even the taxi squad is at one

end of the bench, where it is learning and perhaps praying that next year will see all of its members suited up and ready to play.

The Giants have a system whereby assistant coaches are responsible for individual specialty men — kickers, kickoff squad, and all the others who have a definite, if short-lived, game responsibility.

The whole situation may look like organized confusion to many fans, but

the central control is there. The moral behind all this is to reduce waste, to make every move and every second count in terms of *adding* something to the action that is going on. For example, if Ken

Kavanaugh spots something from his perch high in the stadium, he will be in touch immediately with Griffing, who will in turn tell Sherman or Robustelli or another coach as soon as he can organize the information. It is much like war, I suppose, and the stakes sometimes seem as high.

118

THE TORMENTORS

OVER THE YEARS, the Giants have been particularly bothered by certain players around the league who seem to have their greatest days against New York, spoiling championships in some cases, physically weakening the team in others.

There is a little bit more than some kind of hex to all of this. Don't forget that a good player is generally good most of the time. Of course, if he's a runner, he'll be stopped from time to time — a certain defense will be impossible for him to penetrate, or a certain tackle or linebacker will be literally glued to him all afternoon. If he's a passer, on some days he won't be able to complete a throw for the Scarsdale Little League team — his receivers will drop everything he throws to them as if they were in the employ of some sinister destructive force; onrushing linemen will brush his blockers away like cardboard. But these special competitors have something unique about them: they perform on a slightly different

level against the Giants — always competent, frequently outstanding. A great tormentor is a menace to the whole league — and more deadly than we like to think to the inhabitants of Yankee Stadium. Here are some of my top choices:

Jimmy Brown, Cleveland Browns

A superstar in almost every respect, Brown has wrecked the Giants both in New York and in his home town. I think that Jimmy is the greatest runner of all time. The Giants have had considerable trouble with him, right from the first year he came into the league from Syracuse. This is not a record book, but if it were the list of Brown's feats would force us to include a special section. He has been a leader in rushing, scoring, rushing attempts; most yards gained for one season, individual game and lifetime, and many others. He is one of the few men for whom the term "superstar" can be used legitimately — and not become a cliché. Brown can hurt you both inside and outside. His famous rebellion against what he felt to be the restrictive offense of Paul Brown is well known. When he was given his freedom by Blanton Collier, this young man from Syracuse really began to run wild. He is also a dangerous flare-pass catcher with superb balance and power. If Jim would concentrate more on his blocking, he could perhaps take the heat off his own running efforts when the time came — by upping the morale of the other runner-blockers working with him, as Paul Hornung and Jim Taylor of Green Bay do for each other.

JIMMY BROWN, 32

BOBBY MITCHELL, 49

Bobby Mitchell, Washington Redskins

The Giants often don't know how to stop Bobby. He has great speed, of course, but he's quite a faker, too. He is one of the most elusive men in the NFL, and he's hard for anyone to defense, even the experienced and skillful Giants backfield that has been so effective for so many seasons. Bobby is still young, and will be even more of a thorn in the years to come.

124

Larry Wilson, St. Louis Cardinals

Larry is a gambler, a red-dogging safety man with few equals. He's a floater and a smart one. He has come out of nowhere many times to swipe a pass that some quarterback just couldn't believe could ever fall into alien hands. He is awfully good at sensing where the ball will be at any given moment. Dick Lynch has this quality, too, and I really don't know how you can analyze it. With many good defensive backs, it's an extra sense or two, a hidden eye that makes it possible to cover the football, no matter how many fakes and cuts the offensive receiver or the opposing quarterback give you. As a result of this gambling nature, however, Wilson can have his bad days. He has to. He simply gives a lot away in order to play the way he does. Like the little boy in the story, when he is good, he is very, very good, but when he is bad . . .

LARRY WILSON, 8

Sonny Randle, St. Louis Cardinals

Randle has one of the best sets of hands in the league. I've seen him make some impossible catches against the Giants, in the most impossible situations. He has good speed and outstanding fakes, which often are more of a factor in springing him loose than his raw speed. Some receivers are faster, but few are more sure.

SONNY RANDLE, 88

BUDDY DIAL, 84

Buddy Dial, Dallas Cowboys

Buddy has been around, and has proved his worth many times over. He is one of the most outstanding examples of the real pro — the guy who gets everything possible out of his natural equipment — and then puts out a little more to kill you with it. Dial is not especially fast, as anyone knows who's been watching the NFL since Buddy came to the league. But he has some of the best fakes and moves of anyone catching passes today. He makes a great effort and is a good actor, and stickier fingers never grew anywhere, any time.

128

Tommy McDonald, Dallas Cowboys

Tommy is a natural if there ever was one. He is beautifully equipped to catch a pass — great speed, sure hands, and overwhelming fakes. He has had some torrid days against the Giants. He can murder you deep with that flashing speed, and he has come up with game savers, in the most hallowed journalistic tradition, on more occasions than the Giants would like to remember.

TOMMY McDONALD, 25

John Henry Johnson, Pittsburgh Steelers

This old pro is a consistent star against the Giants, and might be the exception to the general rule we've set on the tormentor's ability to torment anyone — not just the Giants. John Henry might be the one fellow who *really* gets better when he plays New York. He has shown his great desire and power to many a bruised tackler, but he seems to save an extra effort for the Giants. He is another example of the supreme pro: he's got an exceptionally good head on him, and he always knows what he's doing; he hits the hole every time with outstanding balance and power. He has had to work to get where he is today, but he deserves every bit of it. And he's particularly hard to stop when there's a first down within even smelling distance.

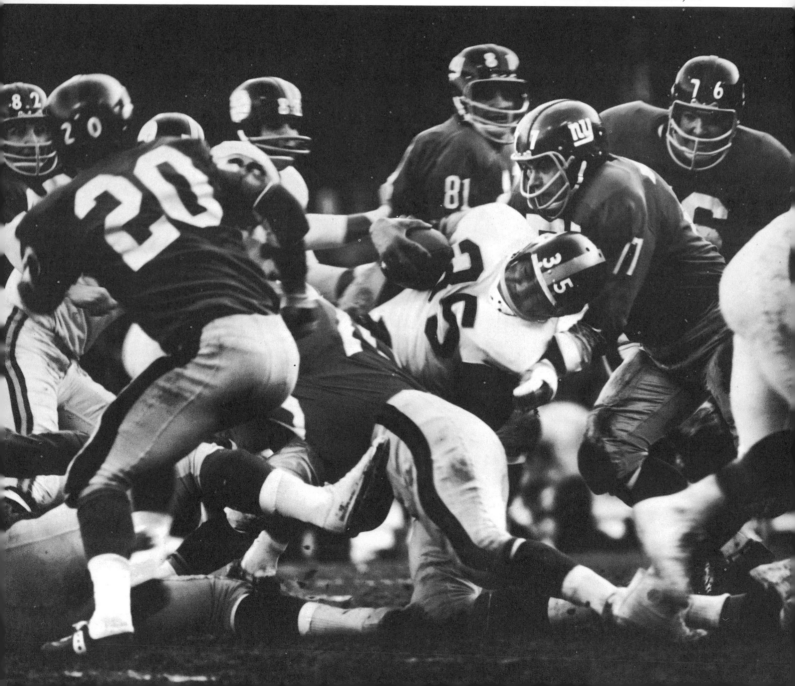

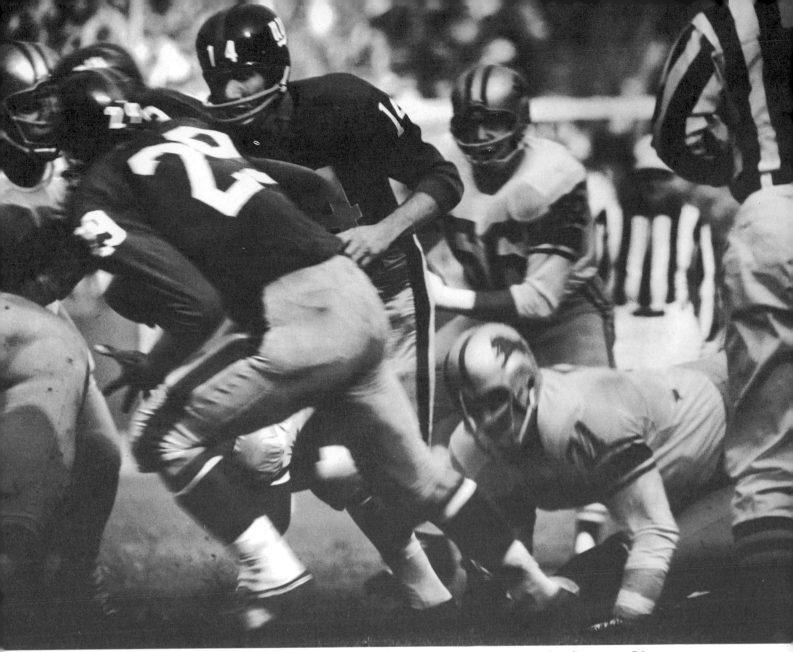

JOE SCHMIDT, 56

Joe Schmidt, Detroit Lions

Although he's not against gambling from time to time, Schmidt has that famous quality of being in the right place at the right time. Joe is also a great team leader, steady and sure of himself, and this confidence inspires his mates. Remember, the Lions have a pretty fair defensive unit. Joe Schmidt also has the reputation of being one of the most vicious tacklers in the NFL. Good head, good body, good spirit — all are pretty hard to beat.

131

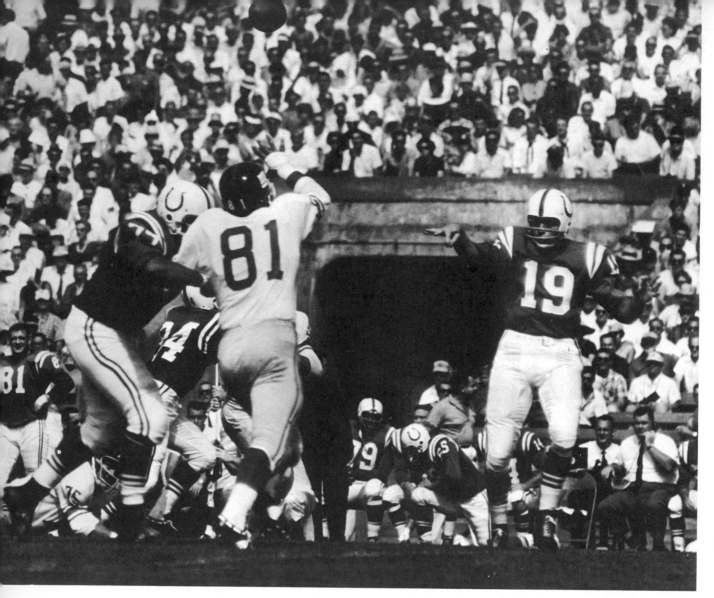

JOHNNY UNITAS, 19

Johnny Unitas, Baltimore Colts

Our tormentors are not listed in order of importance, or obviously this particular one would come very close to the top of the list. Unitas is a consummate professional quarterback. He releases the ball so fast that you can have him halfway down and lo, the ball is *swoosh* into the hands of some loose end for six points. He has deadly fakes — many times a rookie lineman has gone high to block that famous right arm, when around him goes number 19. Johnny is one of the most exciting players in the game today; he'll take tremendous chances and still always play the percentages often enough to come out a consistent winner. He's every bit the gambler Tittle is, if not more so, and just as effective a team leader and inspiration to his entire offense. He can kill you long or short, but his deadliest weapon, of course, is the game breaker, the long pass that seems to fly off his passing hand as if it had eyes.

132

Abe Woodson, San Francisco 49ers

In our section on kickoffs, we talked about this game breaker. He has one of the most electrifying qualities that a back can have: he can come into a mass of bodies at midfield and emerge free and clear — and then go on as if he had

ABE WOODSON, 40

actually been propelled, rather than buffeted, by the contact. Abe has great balance and speed, of course, but he can thread his way through the toughest and tiniest holes. In the most exciting play in football — the kickoff — he is valuable, as we've pointed out, but he is generally a very talented operator who can hurt a team in any number of ways.

There are many other tormentors around the league — and more are joining the number right now. As they continue to gain more experience and skill, the rookies of today will replace the veterans of yesterday. But, for the Giants' sake, I hope they take their time.

Just to show how this particular tormenting sword cuts two ways, how would you like to be a rookie defensive halfback spending an afternoon trying to stop Del Shofner? Or a young safety man coming into Yankee Stadium on a late autumn afternoon, when the shadows get very tricky, trying to bat down a score or more of Y. A. Tittle's most accurate passes? Or how about covering Gifford on a down and out, Walton on a down and in? It's not much fun. A point again worth making: the tormentor is a tormentor to everyone, including himself, when he has a bad day.

Tormenting can be extremely personal, and is not confined to one team against another. The Jim Taylor–Sam Huff rivalry is an honest one. It was blown out of proportion, I think, by certain writers who wanted to add a little spice to their lives.

But it is there. So, too, is the Huff-Brown competition a little keener than most. Huff, when he was with the Giants, had to key on Jimmy whenever the two teams met. Often the whole outcome of the game depended on Sam's ability to diagnose the Cleveland strategy; New York's defense meant containment of Brown — or a lost cause.

Tormentors can be defensed, but they can work very effectively to foil this defense, especially when twin tormentors are in the game at the same time. I've already mentioned how Hornung and Taylor work together for the Packers. By their ferocious blocking, they help each other's morale, and make it doubly hard for any great linebacker, like Huff, to stop both of them. One good block deserves another. Too many backs are great runners and pass catchers, but not good blockers. Their value is in their running and receiving, of course. The coup is to find someone who can do *all* — and many of these men can.

Don't forget that tormenting in the NFL depends on your point of view. Just so we don't give all the credit to backs and ends, consider for a moment a man like Jim Parker of the Colts, who is poison to every man who ever played opposite him. The tormentor has all the moves he needs to be great against the league, even on a bad day, which means, I guess, that he rarely has a bad day, which is why he's such a blasted tormentor.

OFF THE FIELD

SOME YEARS AGO, Irwin Shaw, the well-known novelist, portrayed the classic athlete who never could quite make it in the real world outside the safe confines of the football stadium. Shaw called his story, "The Eighty Yard Run," and it has served as a model for many creative writing classes — and for many football players who, they were soon warned, would end up like Christian Darling (Shaw's non-hero) if they weren't careful.

Football is a physical test, a competition that is unequaled in the everyday world of commerce. It does produce a certain kind of person, one who has been taught to hit, and hit hard. But to end it all there is really quite naive. If a good professional has been able to make it in the NFL for any number of years, you can be sure that he has a fairly well-functioning brain — and that he does know which knife to use.

We've talked about the complexities of the game and its demands. This same kind of discipline is necessary in the life that must be led outside the football milieu, where a man must be able to produce with his skills and his personality more than with his physical speed or his hard head. On top of this is a real desire by most professional football players to contribute something more than hard knocks to the society in which they live. Although it's perhaps unsophisticated in some quarters to say so today, Giants (and most NFL players) do believe in their families and their jobs. They feel themselves to be fortunate, and they want to share this good fortune with their fellow citizens. In fact, I knew a rough and tough college coach who used to refer to his players as citizens, and there were varying degrees: "John is a better citizen this year," this coach used to say, "and we are proud of him." But pride in one's self or in one's job is proved in action. To prove theirs, many of the Giants have been regularly contributing to their communities long before the day they started to play football. They have been given the opportunity to meet a great many people they wouldn't have met otherwise,

136

people who are in many cases influential in their respective professions. But I've never known a steel executive who kept a football player on his payroll because he was fun to throw the football around with, or because he played a great game of golf. The off-season careers of the Giants are serious, and the results of these endeavors have to be real ones — or they don't continue.

The striking thing about the Giants is that at least one third (and this is conservative) of the active squad now makes its home in the New York area. But other clubs have topped this, especially the two California ones; their men are given aptitude tests, counseling according to their special skills and college majors, and then are expected to produce on the jobs that they land. The list of exceptionally successful pros is quite long. It can be regarded as a relatively valid cross-section of all Americans, all doing different jobs, some coming from small towns making it big in the metropolis, others born and reared in the big city and staying there to make a lasting name for themselves long after the arms and legs are best used for signing orders and running for commuter trains.

Some of the examples from the Giants are interesting, I think, and my career in broadcasting and insurance is only one. The chance that Andy Robustelli has — of owning his own business in Stamford, Connecticut — for Frank Gifford to succeed in radio and television, for Kyle Rote to go into active coaching with the Giants and then to become sports director of a major metropolitan radio station, WNEW — all are well known. And it's easy to spot others around who are healthy and happy citizens in their chosen professions and all because they are *good* at their jobs. Of course, the NFL experience helped them, and they are the first to admit that. But no one, including Pete Rozelle, helped them keep their jobs.

One interesting combination, I believe, is the similarity between two quite different players and personalities: Tom Harmon, formerly of the Los Angeles Rams and one of the all-time greats before World War II at the University of Michigan, and Jerry Reichow, the pass-catching end on the Minnesota Vikings and former quarterback for the University of Iowa Hawkeyes.

Harmon is now one of the most successful sportscasters in the nation. He heads a large staff for a major network on the West Coast, and he has grown steadily in this job for almost twenty years. He started with a marvelous opportunity, but he had to produce behind that microphone. Reichow, from the small Iowa town of Decorah, came out of the University of Iowa with a chance that he might never be drafted at all. He was, but soon found that he was not slated to play quarterback. Instead, he learned how to play end, and he has become one of the surest in the business. In the off-season he is a top salesman for a midwestern company, and he admits frankly that his football reputation gets him into almost any place he wants to go. But once the small talk about large football events is over, Jerry has to start talking business fast and well. And he can. But his first opportunity was helped along immeasurably by his ability on the end of a pass. And why not?

Other examples are too many to set down here. But the point is a good one: there is a long life ahead of most professional football players, and they are well equipped to use their experience to

Left to right, DICK PESONEN, AARON THOMAS, DON CHANDLER, JERRY HILLEBRAND, BOB TAYLOR, EDDIE DOVE, ALEX WEBSTER, ANDY BRANCATO — vice-president and general manager, Howard Clothes, JACK MARA — president, New York Giants, JACK SULLIVAN — general manager, WNEW

Left to right, ALEX WEBSTER, Y. A. TITTLE, DON CHANDLER, DEL SHOFNER

make the most of it. If they don't the loss is only theirs.

There are bonuses, though, in this off-season life, and some delightful ones. This past spring, the Giants were given a rather unusual gift by one of the sponsors of the weekly games on WNEW, Howard Clothes. The entire Giants squad and their wives were flown to Puerto Rico to vacation and to contribute to the Physical Fitness Exchange Program that carried

GINGER and JOE WALTON

Don Chandler instructing

Dick Lynch

the blessings of none other than a Texas sports enthusiast named Lyndon Baines Johnson.

Armed with several footballs signed by the President, Giants players took off for the sunny island the first week in May, where they conducted football classes for the youngsters of Puerto Rico (many of whom had never seen a football player before). The kids, for some strange reason, knew Tittle as the Bald Eagle and Don Chandler as Babe. Their reputations had preceded them.

The players had more fun than the kids

AARON THOMAS

did. Also, the wives got a welcome relief from bringing up their own children. Such WNEW stalwarts as William B. Williams and Ted Brown joined in the games, as well as our own Dan Rubin. Marty Glickman did the play-by-play, and I was referee.

Joe Walton, Y. A. Tittle, Don Chandler, Bob Taylor, Dick Lynch, Alex Webster, Del Shofner, Aaron Thomas, Jerry Hillebrand, and many others spent about ten days doing what comes naturally — and piling up a great deal of good will in the bargain. Chandler found some apt

142

JERRY HILLEBRAND and Y. A. TITTLE

punting pupils, Tittle had no need to look far for boys who wanted to learn to throw the football, and Shofner had trouble keeping his defensive cover off his back.

The season now upon us is a short one — especially in terms of one's life work. But the lessons learned and the contacts made are frankly worth nothing if another slightly outworn word isn't made to apply: character. And in this salute, I must say I've never known a Giant without it. If some players somewhere are doomed to studying their old press clippings or picking up dollars signing autographs, I

Del Shofner and Don Chandler

BOB TAYLOR

145

haven't seen much of it — and I don't think I ever will. So Irwin Shaw can come over to Yankee Stadium on any given home Sunday, and we'll compare notes. Color us blue, but a rousing royal blue, if you please. This institution goes first class.

A GLOSSARY OF FOOTBALL TERMS

Professional football has contributed some very special words to the English language. Some of them are still in process of changing, but to help you understand what you're hearing and seeing each Sunday afternoon in the NFL, here are simple explanations of some of the most important terms:

1. **Red Dog:** Linebacker is leaving his accustomed position to rush passer.

2. **Storm:** Two outside linebackers making the same rush at the passer, leaving their spots of responsibility in hopes that this sudden "storm" will confuse the offensive blockers.

3. **Blitz:** All three linebackers are leaving their spots to go after the unfortunate quarterback.

4. **Weak Side:** The side on offense having the fewer number of players, at a given time, on it. In other words, if the Giants take their left halfback and position him on the right side, the right side becomes the strong, and the left the weak side. Giants opponents often defense the Giants against weak-side plays, because the New York running offense often favors this maneuver.

5. **Draw:** A play that begins out of what appears to be a pass. The object is to draw onrushing linemen in, and when they have committed themselves, the quarterback hands off to his fullback or other deep back. Offensive linemen, since they have their opponents sucked in, simply block the rushers the way they are going. Most effective against a tough rushing team.

6. **Screen:** Offensive linemen fake their blocks while the quarterback drops back, fakes a pass, sucking the defensive linemen in; offensive linemen go to their appointed positions to either side of the field or in the middle. Right behind these linemen is a halfback or fullback ready to receive a short pass from the quarterback.

7. **Flare:** Quarterback drops back into his cup; if deep men are covered, he throws to the man going short and wide — or flaring.

8. **Tango:** Maneuver between end and linebacker; most effective in rushing the passer. End has outside responsibility and linebacker protects the inside in the event of a run.

9. **Fold Maneuver:** In a fold tactic, two defensive linemen attempt to confuse the offense by crossing, or folding, one behind the other, and not going straight ahead into the opposing offensive linemen.

10. **Zone Blocking:** In zone-blocking formation, the offensive lineman takes the man straight ahead of him.

11. **Hole Numbering:** Even numbers on line are right side, odd are left, highest numbers at each end, growing smaller as you move toward the center. Backs are numbered one to four. Play example: 48-sweep would be four back to eight hole, or left halfback around right end (see below).

```
7  5  3  2  4  6  8
0  0  0  0  0  0  0
            1
      4     3     2
```

147

DAN RUBIN'S TIPS
FOR PHOTOGRAPHERS

How the pictures in this book can help you shoot better football action.

Frontispiece If I am on the field and want dramatic, yet wide, coverage to tell a story, I use the Wide Angle Hasselblad. I try to keep a figure large in the foreground.

Pages 2-3 In covering a game I sometimes need a key picture to fix the location. Therefore, I used a Veriwide 100L, which is a special, extremely wide-angle camera. This photograph, which has not been cropped, shows the film format.

Page 17 Training camp has its special problems. There is lots going on, and not necessarily for long periods of time. Therefore, I want to shoot as much and as fast as possible. I generally use a Contarex with an assortment of lenses; in this case, a 50mm. lens set at 1/25th of a second to give some movement.

Page 23 This picture was also taken with a Contarex, but with a 35mm. lens. A white card reflector or a low power flash unit could have been used, but I was looking for a mood rather than portraits of players, which the reflector or flash would have given me.

Page 38 Again the Rolleiflex was used, this time to give a wide field, yet without the necessity for a super-wide camera. I use Tri-X film pushed to ASA 650 with available light, because any flash in snow or rain will not be effective.

Page 30 A Rolleiflex with a 200-watt-second Ascor strobe unit was used for this photograph. The right-from-the-floor angle adds drama and power.

Page 47 I generally work with a Novoflex-Noflexar F9 640mm. lens on my Hasselblad on a tripod. Hanging from my neck is a Rolleiflex set at 20 feet, f/11 at the fastest shutter speed possible in relation to available light. In this case I was shooting Tittle throwing a pass, with my 640mm. lens. I sensed that the ball and Shofner were coming in my direction, so I grabbed my Rollei and shot from the hip.

Pages 36-37 On the sidelines, the Rolleiflex — my utility camera — is used for just about everything but long-range action. Here I have shot wide open to center the interest on the pregame huddle.

Page 51 Quite often the peak action of a particular play is at the far side of the field. Naturally I want to get as close as possible, so I use the 640mm. lens. A longer lens might be good, but I have found that this particular length is the best for football; anything longer, in most cases, is just too tight.

Page 58 Here again I have used the Novoflex 640mm. at its widest opening – f/9 – this time to concentrate on Tittle. I have told the story of the action, yet by selective focus I have made my point.

Page 61 Panning with a 640mm. Novoflex is best done from the tripod with its horizontal swing completely loose. This photograph was taken at 1/10th of a second while making a sweeping pan as Webster charged through the line.

Page 65 A photographer, to get good sports action, must have at least a fair knowledge of the game he's shooting. I find it essential to move around the field as play progresses, hoping to anticipate the quarterback and be where he is sending the play. As an example, had I not been in the proper position, it would have been impossible to take this picture. I used the Hasselblad at 1/500th, with the 640mm. Novoflex to stop this action.

Page 73 An important part of sports photography is the use of what you have in your frame. Here I have a full-length shot of Tittle passing, which is effective to tell a particular story. But in the second photo, printed from the same negative and shown at the start of this section, I have cropped in tight to dramatize the quarterback in action.

Page 67 Here is an example of a lens being almost too long. This is the full negative area from the Hasselblad with the 640mm. Novoflex. The Giants were on their own goal line and I was on the end line, unable to move back; I was, therefore, just about ten yards behind Tittle. In this case, though, the picture is successful, but I would not like to be this tight in all my shots.

150

Page 98 Cropping while shooting is also important. In this case I composed a particular photo in my mind, and when the kickoff took place I was focused on the kicking tee.

Page 118 The Mara luck with good weather is not always good luck to me, as I get some of my most dramatic photographs on a muddy field. On a particularly bad day, Sam Huff plowed up ten yards of Yankee Stadium sod with his helmet, and I caught him with my Rolleiflex when he came to the bench.

Page 119 There are many things at a football game that tell the story other than the action on the field. In this case, I photographed one of the equipment bags in front of the telephone table. I used available light with my Rolleiflex at f/3.5 to keep the background soft and not distracting.

Page 122 I only occasionally shoot from the stands; I feel that the most dynamic action can be obtained at ground level. For the fan in the seats I recommend the longest lens he can afford or the Mirrotar f/4.5 500mm., made by Carl Zeiss. It's a good choice because its mirrored optical system allows for a lens under ten inches long, where an ordinary 500mm. lens might be three feet long and would obviously bother the fans in the next row. In this picture I used the Mirrotar on my Contarex camera.

152